OPPOSING VIEWPOINTS SERIES

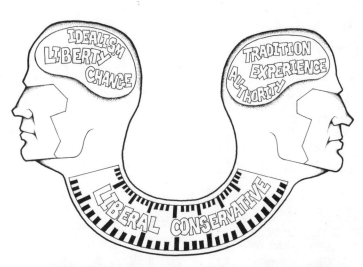

LIBERALS AND CONSERVATIVES

A DEBATE ON THE WELFARE STATE

DAVID L. BENDER
(Editor)

Greenhaven Press Inc. — 1611 Polk St. N.E., Mpls., MN 55413

New revised and extended edition

© COPYRIGHT 1971, 1973 by GREENHAVEN PRESS

ISBN 0-912616-08-3 PAPER EDITION
ISBN 0-912616-26-1 CLOTH EDITION

TABLE OF CONTENTS

56001 Page

JC
571
B4
L5

TABLE OF CONTENTS

TABLE OF EXERCISES

THE POLITICAL SPECTRUM

AND THE WELFARE STATE

Reactionary

Conservative

Liberal

Radical

THE POLITICAL SPECTRUM

The terms, liberal, conservative, radical, extremist and a few similar labels, are perhaps used more than any others in social studies classes, in political converations and by the communications media. However, it is doubtful that many people have a clear understanding of these terms and the differences they signify. It is difficult to pick up the editorial page of any newspaper without reading about the in-fighting of the liberals and conservatives in either the House or the Senate. One is also likely to read about radical or reactionary groups or interests at work somewhere in our society. Because these terms are so often and so carelessly used, it is important that the interested student and the concerned citizen be able to define them and recognize when they are properly used.

Although this volume presents a comparison of extreme viewpoints on the political spectrum, it is first necessary to compare mainstream liberalism and conservatism so that a sense of perspective may be gained in approaching the far left and the far right.

One may distinguish between liberals and conservatives in two ways: (1) their readiness to change, (2) their philosophical differences. Let us first consider their readiness to accept or bring about change.

READINESS TO CHANGE

If one were to construct a continuum showing the reaction to change, the following stopping points would be noted:

THE POLITICAL SPECTRUM

Radicals	Liberals	Conservatives	Reactionaries

Left Wing	Right Wing

Radicals and liberals are called left-wingers or leftists and welcome change. Conservatives and reactionaries are called right-wingers or rightists and are quite reluctant to accept change. If each position on the continuum were defined it would read as follows:

2

The Radical	He favors a radical or basic change. He is quite impatient and would quickly support a revolution to bring about the desired change.
The Liberal	He is ready to move forward and accept change but would be considered a reformer rather than a revolutionary.
The Conservative	He is quite content with things the way they are.
The Reactionary	He wants change also, but wants to retreat into the past and restore the order of things the way they used to be.

A former advisor of Franklin D. Roosevelt's, Rexford Tugwell, skillfully uses the example of a community's need for a new train station to illustrate the difference between liberals and radicals: *"Liberals would like to rebuild the station while the trains are running; radicals prefer to blow up the station and forego service until the new structure is built."*[1] One might add that conservatives would prefer to keep the old station, being satisfied with it, while reactionaries would abandon the station entirely since they do not approve of trains in the first place.*

I believe that liberals tend to design houses, conservatives to build them. The liberal mind, by and large, moves more quickly than the conservative's to original thought.

Those of us on the right tend to stand by tradition, precedent, and the old ways of doing things.

James J. Kilpatrick, Conservative Commentator

Whatever the differences between the left-wing and the right-wing in accepting change, all four viewpoints are helpful to society. The radical points out the future's

[1] Rexford G. Tugwell, **The Industrial Discipline and the Governmental Arts** (New York: Columbia University Press, 1934-5), p. 229.

*In this hypothetical situation, the reader must consider the need for a new train station and the method of building it open to question, otherwise the liberal solution would appear to be the only prudent one.

possibilities while the liberal helps to see them realized through the practice of compromise. The conservative cautions us to preserve past accomplishments and the reactionary reminds us of our heritage and the glory of times past.

PHILOSOPHICAL DIFFERENCES

More important than their readiness to change are the philosophical differences that separate left-wingers and right-wingers. The greatest areas of disagreement concern the nature of man, reliance on tradition and individual freedom.

1. THE NATURE OF MAN

Liberals generally approach man with a great deal of optimism. They feel he is basically good, and though he may be born ignorant he is not evil. They do not believe in original sin and as a consequence they feel man can be perfected by education and knowledge. If you give him an opportunity to better himself he will take advantage of it and improve. Conservatives, on the other hand, have a rather pessimistic opinion of man. Because they believe he has been tainted by original sin they expect less of man. They are reluctant to provide welfare programs such as aid to dependent mothers or unemployment compensation because they do not think it will be used properly, and in fact feel it will cause additional problems because the weaker side of man's nature will be reinforced. Liberals welcome reforms because they feel that man's history is one of continual progress as he informs and improves himself.

Liberals also favor rapid movement toward constitutional or democratic forms of government because of their great confidence in the ability of the enlightened citizen to make wise and prudent choices at the ballot box. Conservatives are a little more suspicious of the average citizen's ability to direct a government, even only indirectly as in a representative democracy such as the United States.[2]

[2] American government was partially founded on the concept of direction for the masses by an enlightened minority. The founding fathers, while meeting at the Constitutional Convention in Philadelphia in 1787, made provisions for this practice in the new constitution. Various methods were devised to place the reins of government in the hands of the better educated and more responsible members of American

4

2. TRADITION AND REFORM

The second philosophical difference between liberals and conservatives, reliance on tradition, is somewhat related to their readiness to change. One of the fundamental values of conservatism is a confidence in the accumulated wisdom and values of the past. Conservatives do not favor quick change for they feel that it can bring nothing but negative results. The positive accomplishments of man have been the result of gradual change and slow growth. They do not, like liberals, advocate utopian forms of government, for they are skeptical of man improving his condition greatly in a short period of time. Conservatives represent the status quo, which they consider the end result of centuries of experience and knowledge. Conservatives feel little need to articulate their philosophy for it represents the system that presently exists. Liberals, on the other hand, impatient for improvement, are constantly presenting arguments and programs to change the on-going system. This explains why the liberal journals of opinion outnumber those of a conservative persuasion. Whereas **The National Review** may be said to present the conservative viewpoint, **The New Republic, The Progressive** and **The Nation** all speak for liberalism.

Russell Kirk, a conservative spokesman, defines tradition as a set of *"received opinions, conviction religious and moral and political and aesthetic passed down from generation to generation, so that they are accepted by most men as a matter of course."*[3] Conservatives are satisfied to live with tradition; liberals are anxious to question established opinions and convictions, whether they be religious, moral, political or aesthetical.

3. AUTHORITY AND INDIVIDUAL FREEDOM

Closely allied to the difference of opinion on the importance of tradition is the disagreement over authority

society:
1. The creation of the Senate as a check on the House of Representatives with members given six year terms to give them a greater degree of independence.
2. The election of state senators by state legislators rather than by the general voting public.
3. The election of the President by electors rather than by the general voting public.

[3] Russell Kirk, *Prescription, Authority, and Ordered Freedom,* **What Is Conservatism,** ed. Frank S. Meyer (New York: Holt, Rinehart & Winston, 1964), p. 27.

versus individual freedom. Because liberals expect man to act correctly when he is informed they would give him a great amount of liberty in his actions. Conservatives however, not having such an optimistic opinion of man, feel that he must often be controlled and directed for his own good.

A partial understanding of the disagreement on the topic of individual freedom as opposed to institutionalized authority can be gained by simply defining the terms liberalism and conservatism. Liberalism is derived from the early nineteenth century Spanish political party, the *"Liberales",* a party that advocated a constitutional form of government that would grant more freedom to individuals than the established authoritarian government it was opposing. The word *"liberal"* has since come to signify any idea, movement, or party that favors granting more individual liberty than the traditional authoritarian forms of government normally permit. The term *"conservatism"* means literally to conserve, namely the traditions, customs and governments that have evolved through many generations of human experience.

Again, because of the liberal's optimistic outlook, he believes that man will use wisely any liberties given him. The conservative, however, believes that man must be somewhere restrained and guided by those in society who are better educated and better equipped to govern. Edmund Burke, who has been called the father of modern conservatism, expresses the conservative's aversion to giving too much freedom to the individual:

> The extreme of liberty . . . obtains nowhere, nor ought to obtain anywhere; because extremes, as we all know, in every point which relates either to our duties or satisfactions in life, are destructive both to virtue and enjoyment. Liberty, too, must be limited in order to be possessed. [4]

It must be obvious to the reader that the philosophical differences that separate liberals and conservatives spring from their basic disagreement on human nature and its perfectibility. One could cite other philosophical arguments

[4] Ross J.S. Hoffman and Paul Levack (eds.), **Burke's Politics: Selected Writings and Speeches of Edmund Burke** (New York: Alfred A. Knopf, Inc., 1949), p. 109.

such as the equality of all men, rationalism versus tradition, intellectual freedom and censorship, the role and scope of government and the nature of religion, topics that all cause a direct confrontation between liberals and conservatives. But at the root of all of these disagreements is the central question concerning the nature of man, his basic goodness and perfectability and his evil strain and tendency toward weakness and selfishness.

THE NATURE OF EXTREMISM

For purposes of discussion and clarity right-wing extremist groups will henceforth be referred to as the far right and left-wing extremists groups as the radical left. The far right organizations are extreme conservative groups because they do not wish to merely conserve existing social, religious and political institutions but would rather return to the customs and institutions of an earlier age. Conversely, radical groups are not interested in reforming society in a piecemeal fashion, they would rather confront the establishment with a revolution, bloody if necessary, to bring about the kind of society they envision. Before looking at the characteristics that are peculiar to reactionaries and radicals respectively, it would be helpful to consider some characteristics which they have in common.

1. Extreme Measures. They recommend extreme measures in dealing with domestic and world problems, for they see a deep void between good and evil, and evil must be dealt with forcefully and immediately. The art of compromise, upon which the American system of government is founded, and a practice much used by mainstream liberals and conservatives, is derided as giving in to evil forces, whether it be the forces of communism or the establishment.

2. The Anti-Movement. Related to the first characteristic of dividing the world into two opposing forces, the forces of good and evil, is the tendency to be anti something. It may be an anti-communistic, anti-Semitic, anti-U.N., anti-Negro, or anti-white philosophy. The life giving power in many fringe groups is their hatred or fear of some racial group, governmental agency or movement in society to which they attribute a great number if not all of society's problems.

3. A Tendency to Disregard Civil Liberties and Laws in the Name of the Cause. Because they are convinced of the purity of their causes, and the evilness of those they oppose, drastic means are often justified by their goals. The far right has decided to fight fire with fire by adopting the tactics of the communists they oppose. They also favor an emphasis on giving police officials more power in dealing with society's enemies before the courts of the land when this power conflicts with individual civil liberties. Radicals frequently break laws to direct public attention to their programs and goals, and show little regard for the legal authority of police officials whom they often call pigs. In general, innocent bystanders may be hurt by both the far right and the radical left as an unfortunate but unavoidable consequence of pursuing their goals.

1. CHARACTERISTICS OF THE FAR RIGHT

In addition to the characteristics it shares with the radical left, the far right can be identified by its own set of general traits.

1. An avid anti-communist sentiment, directed at communists within the United States and those abroad, is one of the most noticeable features of the far right. For the greater part of this century the far right has felt that American government and society have been under attack by communists who have been quite successful in influencing American foreign and domestic policy. The far right differs from conservatives on this point in that the far right believes that a worldwide conspiracy involving American communists and communist sympathizers is instrumental in bringing about the communization of the United States through socialistic economic and social programs. Conservatives, however, would attribute American softness on communism to the mistakes of Democratic presidential administrations over the last thirty years.

2. The far right is also concerned about the decline of traditional moral values. Many members of the far right belong to fundamentalist religious denominations to which the term *"new morality"* is anathema.

3. The far right has traditionally been loyal to the Republican party.

4. Programs and movements they are opposed to they label as communist-inspired, whether it be the civil rights movement, fluoridation of city water or long hair.

5. The far right is concerned about the corrupting influence of the United States Supreme Court on American society. Specifically, they are dissatisfied with decisions regulating prayers in public schools, decisions recognizing the constitutional rights of accused individuals and decisions that in any way increase the power of the federal government.

6. The far right opposes government programs on the basis that the less the government does the harder it will be for the communists to take over.

7. The United Nations is also seen as a socialistic tool, being used by the Communists to enslave the world, and they urge the United States to withdraw from it.

8. The far right is not optimistic about federal legislation solving our racial problems and instead calls for a personal change of heart by individual citizens.

9. When legal action is necessary to solve problems of social unrest and disorder the far right would call on law enforcement agencies first.

10. The far right favors a capitalistic system as opposed to any form of socialism.*

2. CHARACTERISTICS OF THE RADICAL LEFT

The radical left has changed its complexion considerably during the decade of the 1960's. Daniel Boorstin presents a clear picture of pre-1960 members of the radical left.

The Depression Decade beginning in 1929 saw in the United States a host of radicalisms, perhaps more numerous and more influential than any earlier period of our history. Many of these were left-wing movements, which included large numbers of our academics, intellectuals, and men of

---

*Socialism is an economic system that calls for government ownership of basic industries, whereas capitalism is an economic system based on private ownership of property and private enterprise engaged in for profit.

public conscience who became members or fellow travelers of groups dominated by Marxist ideas. They favored a reconstruction of American life on a base of socialism or communism. They had a great deal to do with promoting a new and wider American labor movement, with helping F.D.R. popularize the need for a welfare state, and with persuading Americans to join the war to stop Hitler. Although they fenced in American social scientists by new orthodoxies, they did have a generally tonic effect on American society. However misguided were many of the policies they advocated, these radicals did awaken and sensitize the American conscience. They confronted Americans with some facts of life which had been swept under the rug.[5]

Boorstin claims that the radicals of the past were identified by three characteristics: (1) a search for some kind of new meaning whether in religious, social or economic programs. (2) A *"specific content"*, a philosophy, a program, etc. (3) An allegiance to a common cause; improvement of American society (an affirmation of community as Boorstin puts it).

The radical left of the present is identified by different traits than those of the past.

1. Most left wing groups advocate a socialist form of economy. Some groups feel this goal can be realized democratically through the ballot box. Others are more pessimistic and feel a violent revolution is necessary.

2. Historically the left's underlying theme of socialism has lacked a broad appeal in America which accounts for its small following. However, socialism does seem to have more appeal for young people.

3. The new left is anti-materialistic. It is bored with the affluent society and is not too interested in improving its economic situation. The economic considerations that motivated their parents do not seem to be as important to the young members of the new left.

4. Although they readily condemn the ills of the present system and would tear it down if these ills are not cured, they do not suggest workable alternatives.

---

[5] Daniel J. Boorstin, *The New Barbarians*, **Esquire,** October, 1968, p. 159.

5. They are driven by a sense of idealism that permits few compromises and generates a feeling of elitism.

6. The new left is not too concerned about the communist menace that troubles the far right and would point out that before Americans can condemn communists out of hand they muśt first solve their own domestic problems.

7. The new left advocates *"participatory democracy"* which means that workers and students and the poor should participate in making decisions that effect them.

8. The new left identifies with neither the Republican nor the Democratic party.

9. Ideological differences often prevent unity on the radical left and hence one finds many left wing political organizations.

The characteristics of the radical left and the far right that have been listed are general characteristics. They may not apply to all extremist organizations but they should help the reader gain some insight into the philosophical and operational traits that make both the far right and the radical left uniquely different.

THE DANGER OF LABELING

Before approaching the readings in this volume the reader must be cautioned about labeling a group or an individual as a liberal, a reactionary or whatever the case may be. A group may have what would be considered a liberal position on censorship of pornography but may at the same time hold a conservative position on the question of socialized medicine for the United States. How would you then classify this group, right-wing or left-wing? Although a general conclusion may be reached about the positioning of a specific group on the political spectrum, one must always be careful about irrevocably labeling a group as a reactionary, conservative, liberal or radical group. Individually, almost every person can be positioned at every stopping point on the political spectrum. One would have to conduct a long search to find a person who is a one hundred percent radical and demands a revolution for every cause, or a liberal who is completely dissatisfied with the status quo. The search would be equally fruitless if one were to look for the complete conservative who is satisfied with everything as it is or the reactionary who wants to retreat totally into the past.

It should be clear in the following readings that a group can more or less be positioned at a particular point on the political spectrum and that many organizations leave no doubt as to how they should be labeled. The careful reader should exercise some caution before deciding the political persuasion of a particular group.

1. THE INDIVIDUAL AND THE SPECTRUM

The average American seems to be a bit puzzled in his use of the terms liberal and conservative, and how he would identify himself. A few years ago, the Harris Survey asked a cross section of the public to classify positions on several major policy questions.[6] For each question, persons were asked if they felt a particular stand on the issue was "conservative" or "liberal." The results were as follows:

Position on Issue	Liberal	Conservative
1. "abolition of welfare and making people who collect it go to work"	20%	40%
2. "stop being permissive with student protesters"	22	46
3. "getting tougher on the subject of law and order"	23	48
4. "help blacks move faster toward equality"	54	17
5. "increasing federal programs to help the poor"	51	19
6. "increase spending on air and water pollution control"	41	26
7. "giving corporations a better tax break"	32	29

[6] Louis Harris, *Conservative, Liberal Tags Sometimes Puzzle Public,* **The Minneapolis Star,** January 18, 1971. Reprinted with permission from The Chicago Tribune — N.Y. News Syndicate and the Harris Survey.

8. "doing away with the union shop"	30	27
9. "a system of wage and price controls to curb inflation"	38	23

The survey reveals what positions most Americans believe to be conservative (positions 1-3), which are considered liberal (positions 4-6) and the controversies that Americans experience difficulty in distinguishing between liberal and conservative positions (positions 7-9).

The Harris Survey also showed that a person tends to identify a given stand on an issue in relationship to his own position on the political spectrum. For example, liberals tend to see advocacy or increased spending for air and water pollution programs as a clearly liberal stand, but conservatives see it as an expression of their own political philosophy.

2. THE SHIFT LEFT WITH TIME

In terms of change, society is constantly moving left on the spectrum, as suggested social reforms become adopted programs.

A good example of this occurrence is the advocacy of social security payments for elderly Americans. If one had advocated such payments in 1900, he probably would have been called a radical by his contemporaries for asking for such a significant change in our social and economic structures. If this individual would have advocated the same program in 1935, when the Roosevelt administration pushed through the Social Security Act making it a reality, he probably would have been called a liberal on the issue. If he were to maintain the same position on the issue in the 1950's, long after the social security program was adopted and accepted by the public, he could have been called a conservative for supporting the status quo. By 1973, the original social security program had been expanded by additional benefits and larger pension payments. If our hypothetical individual were to advocate a return to the smaller program he supported back in 1900, he would be called a reactionary for wanting to return to the past.

(At age 14) "They ought to do more for pensioners."

(Age 24) "Pensioners? Yes, but can we afford it?"

(Age 34) "I agree, but higher pensions mean higher taxes."

(Age 44) "More for pensioners? Certainly, but what would it cost?"

(Age 54) "We'd all like pensions to be raised, but . . ."

(Age 64) "They ought to do more for pensioners."

The shift left with time is a partial explanation for the generation gap. Older people tend to be more conservative than the young. Many old people are most comfortable with the ideas and customs acquired during their earlier years. There is some truth to the adage "you can't teach an old dog new tricks." On the other hand, the young are quick to try new clothing and hair styles, new music and other entertainment innovations, and they are more likely to challenge sexual mores and other societal customs. Also, one would be hard pressed to find large numbers of older people demonstrating with the young in the streets against "the establishment."

14

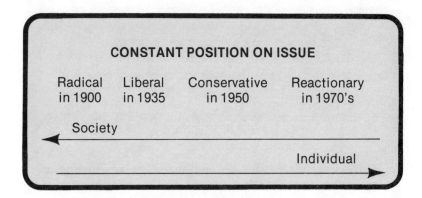

CONSTANT POSITION ON ISSUE

Radical in 1900	Liberal in 1935	Conservative in 1950	Reactionary in 1970's

Society ◄——————————————————————

——————————————————————► Individual

THE WELFARE STATE

DEFINING TERMS

When one examines the welfare state it may be wise to begin by defining terms, for the welfare state issue often triggers an emotional response that can easily cloud its description. One should be careful not to equate socialism and communism with the welfare state, for they are not synonymous terms.

Perhaps one of the clearest descriptions of the welfare state is presented by Arthur J. Schlesinger, Jr., a historian and member of the Kennedy administration:

> Briefly, it is a system wherein government agrees to underwrite certain levels of employment, income, education, medical aid, social security, and housing for all its citizens. The government does not try to do all these things itself; it seeks where possible to supplement the initiatives of private society. But it does accept the ultimate responsibility of guaranteeing "floors" in certain crucial areas, below which it conceives tolerable living to be impossible. And it will intervene when private society demonstrates its incapacity to maintain these minimum standards.[7]

[7]Arthur J. Schlesinger, Jr., *The Welfare State*, **Reporter**, October 11, 1949, p. 28.

ARGUMENTS FOR
THE WELFARE STATE

1. Economic equality is the foundation on which basic freedoms rest. The welfare state can insure a basic economic equality for everyone.

2. Society has a moral responsibility to provide a minimum subsistence level for those citizens who are not able to provide it for themselves.

3. The welfare state represents a "compromise system" midway between an authoritarian government that satisfies everyone's minimum economic needs and a capitalistic system that leaves this task solely to the individual's initiative and ability.

4. Most western democracies have already developed an advanced welfare state. The march of history indicates it is inevitable that the United States also expand its welfare programs.

5. The continued economic growth of the United States economy is dependent on an expanded welfare economy. The welfare state makes consumers out of individuals who would otherwise make no contributions to our economy.

6. The sickness of any member of a society will adversely affect the whole society. For this reason it is in society's best interests to help individuals in need of assistance.

7. To ask for and receive charity is a degrading psychological experience. It is better for individuals to receive help through a government insurance program in a more anonymous fashion.

8. Our technological society, which finds millions of citizens dependent on large corporations and economic conditions beyond their control for their livelihood, should provide financial assistance when people find themselves victimized by the system through unemployment, expensive hospital care, nursing homes that few people can afford, etc.

ARGUMENTS AGAINST THE WELFARE STATE

1. The government has no right to give away the tax dollars of hard working people to those who are unable or unwilling to work.

2. Individual citizen's qualities of initiative and ambition will be destroyed in a "something for nothing society."

3. Local governments and private charities are better able to resolve welfare problems because of their nearness to these problems, than is the distant federal government.

4. The welfare state may destroy our capitalistic system that has made America rich and powerful, and the land of opportunity for millions of immigrants.

5. The welfare state is incompatible with democracy and may lead to socialism or communism, or some other form of totalitarian government.

6. The welfare state will foster an immense bureaucratic monster that will be buried in its own red tape.

7. Not only will the welfare state bring about a loss of personal responsibility and individual initiative, it will also do psychological harm when large numbers of people suffer a lack of pride in accomplishment because of work they have not done.

8. The welfare state will dispense aid and assistance in an impersonal and bureaucratic manner. It is preferable that people receive help from private charities on a person to person basis.

9. Welfare programs once established will be difficult to remove, even though they prove to be ineffective and perhaps harmful to our society.

The welfare state, as one can see from this definition, is a society in which the government takes upon itself the responsibility of seeing that its citizens' economic needs are met, primarily by prodding the private sector of the economy into providing for them. As a last resort, the government, through its own resources and powers, will directly satisfy these needs.

Socialism, on the other hand, is a system of public ownership and management of the means of production, capital, land and property by the state. Private enterprise is nonexistent in the completely socialized state, as all workers are employees of the government.

Communism is similar to socialism in structure, with the difference that it advocates an eventual classless society, an utopian ideal that government will eventually become unnecessary and wither away, leaving a perfect society.

THE WELFARE CONTROVERSY

**"IT IS PERFECTLY TRUE THAT THAT GOVERN-
MENT IS BEST WHICH GOVERNS LEAST. IT IS
EQUALLY TRUE THAT THAT GOVERNMENT IS BEST
WHICH PROVIDES MOST."[8]**

The above statement by Lippman aptly describes the essence of the welfare state controversy. Some believe that the government has the obligation to provide the basic necessities of life for every citizen, and that citizens have a right to expect such assistance. Others claim that government's only responsibility is to provide an environment in which citizens can provide for themselves. This debate is centuries old, but it takes on added significance in an affluent society such as ours, where the government has the resources to conduct a highly developed welfare state. After reading the various arguments presented in the following pages of this book, you should be able to develop an informed opinion of your own.

---

[8] Walter Lippman, **A Preface to Politics**, (New York: Mitchell Kennerley, 1913), p. 266

THE MORAL CASE
FOR THE WELFARE STATE

by Paul Kurtz*

Paul Kurtz is the editor of **The Humanist**, a bi-monthly journal published for the American Humanist Association and the American Ethical Union.

Consider these questions as you read:

1. Why does the author claim we have a moral obligation to help the poor and the needy?
2. What proof does the author present to back up his claim that the arguments against social welfare are incorrect?

*Paul Kurtz, *An End to Poverty: The Moral Case for a New Federal Approach to Welfare*, **The Humanist**, January/February 1971, pp. 5-6. This article first appeared in **The Humanist** January/February 1971, and is reprinted by permission.

POVERTY INTOLERABLE

Poverty and hunger are no longer tolerable in the United States. A society that possesses the means sufficient to satisfy the basic life-needs of all its citizens and does not do so is morally deficient. America's Gross National Product exceeds one trillion dollars, yet we permit poverty and hunger to persist. Surely no one should be allowed to go hungry while others bask in luxury. We spend lavishly on pet foods, and some 30 million Americans still remain "dirt poor," unable to achieve even a minimum standard of living. Until America can realize the levels of aspiration and hope of its disadvantaged, she will suffer the strains of moral disparity between our professed democratic ideals and the actual conditions of human life. Can we solve the problem? It is clear that we must, and that every effort must be expended to do so.

Reprinted with Permission of Sawyer Press, L.A., CA.

"THE-WORLD-OWES-ME-A-LIVING" CRITICISM

One method of mitigating and overcoming at least some of the deprivations of the poor is by means of social welfare. The moral principle upon which social welfare is based, namely, that society has an obligation to help those who cannot help themselves, is a principle that surely should not be in need of defense today. Yet the principle has come under heavy criticism from those who find a conflict between it and the principle of "self-help." It is widely believed by critics that large numbers of public welfare recipients are not entitled to aid since they "refuse to improve their own lot." Middle America views the recipients of welfare like the fabled good-for-nothing grasshopper, who danced and played, singing "the world owes me a living" while the industrious ants were busy working to prepare for the hard winter to come. The protestant ethic emphasizes thrift and hard work as moral virtues, and welfare is seen as an abandonment of the work ethic. Welfarites loaf, it is said, while others toil.

SOCIAL WELFARE DEFENDED

No one can deny the desirability of having productive, gainfully employed citizens, capable of supporting themselves without resort to "public handouts." Yet most of the arguments against public welfare are fallacious. At present some 12.2 million people receive some form of public assistance. But the lion's share goes to dependent children under 18, the aged, the handicapped, disabled, blind, or those unable to work. The truth is, there is only a small percentage of able-bodied employable males who receive welfare (no more than 5 to 10 per cent of the total relief rolls). Many persons are unemployable because of rapid changes in technology and automation, over which they have no control. Although modern technology offers gains, it also entails serious risks. This is especially acute for older workers whose occupational skills are no longer required by social production. Thus often only public remedies can help to resolve the problem of economically marginal people.

Critics complain about the "welfare racket." Undoubtedly there are some flagrant violations, for every system has its imperfections. Yet many in the high-income tax brackets who commiserate with one another about "welfare graft" often are the most skillful in underreporting income and overreporting tax deductions. By and large, welfare support goes to those who genuinely need it. Even those who are

21

unemployed and receive welfare, generally, do so for the short period of time until they can find new employment. Most people would prefer to work rather than receive welfare indefinitely. Human dignity has strong roots in our self-appraisal. The fact that millions of Americans receive public assistance in the form of social security, unemployment payments, or veteran's benefits is often overlooked, for these are considered to be less distasteful than welfare. . . .

REORDERING OF NATIONAL PRIORITIES

The United States as the richest nation in the world spends less of its Gross National Product on welfare than do most other industrial nations. The real challenge that we face is whether in the 1970's we can eliminate the scourge of poverty and thus restore faith in America.

WELFARE
A NATIONAL PROBLEM

Clearly, since welfare is a national problem it should be dealt with by the national government. Obviously, the federal government is in the best position to solve both the human and the fiscal aspects of this problem by taking over the entire welfare responsibility on the basis of establishing national standards and paying the full costs.

At the very least, the federal government could help alleviate the critical fiscal problems of state and local governments through realistic federal revenue sharing.

From a speech by Governor Nelson Rockefeller of New York.

22

THE DANGER OF WELFARISM

by America's Future*

America's Future is a weekly review published by America's Future, Incorporated, which describes itself "as a non-profit, educational organization dedicated to the American form of constitutional government, our free enterprise economy, and opposition to all forms of collectivism."

As you read consider the following questions:

1. Why does the author of this reading feel it would be a mistake for the national government to take over the country's welfare program?
2. What adverse effect does the author claim welfare can have on the integrity of welfare recipients?

*Welfarism, **America's Future**, February 26, 1971, pp. 2-5. Reprinted with permission from **America's Future, Incorporated.**

WELFARISM

England has become a Welfare State, with nationally financed "security" from the cradle to the grave which, bringing Great Britain close to bankruptcy, is turning out to be no security at all. In other words, England as a Welfare State now faces the inevitable consequences of the beguiling but insidious notion that from governments — not from individual efforts of free citizens — all good things flow, such as health, welfare, education, even happiness, with no one paying the bills.

WE, THE PEOPLE

WELFARE STATE
CRADLE TO GRAVE "SECURITY"

7-28-65   FRED O. SEIBEL.

"MERRILY WE ROLL ALONG"

But we in America are the last ones who should look down at England's plight, for we, too, have been building the Welfare State. We haven't gone as far as England but if our own socialist-minded do-gooders have their way, we could find ourselves on a disaster-course to the complete Welfare State.

This matter of rising welfare costs and numbers is very much on the minds of state and city politicians, because it is welfare costs which have brought many of our cities and states to the point of severe financial crisis. The only solution some of these politicians can think of is to dump the whole problem in the lap of the national government — the city politicians demand that the state take over; the state politicians in turn demand that the national government take over. In many cases, of course, what they really mean is that the national government should supply the money, but they'll keep on administering it, as though the national government had some sort of bottomless barrel out of which the money would come. It would come, as it always must, where all our local, state and national government money comes from: from our taxpaying earners.

The solutions to what many call "the welfare mess" are not easy ones and we do not pretend to know exactly what they are. But a good many experts in the field, bearing in mind that part of the mess comprises the entrenched welfare bureaucracies in the states and cities, do question whether the solution lies in replacing or adding to those bureaucracies with a single giant federal bureaucracy. The national government already is deeply involved in various forms of welfarism and the results, in the eyes of these authorities, are far from happy ones. For example, the State of Nevada, faced with mounting welfare costs, made a door-to-door check on welfare recipients. The result was the removal of 3,000 people — 22 percent of those receiving welfare in the state — from the welfare rolls and the saving to the state of a million dollars a year. The State Welfare Director said these people had been cheating the taxpayers out of this sum because of a federal regulation that allows people to get on welfare simply by saying they met the qualifications.

> **This is one of the great evils of welfarism...it transforms the individual from a dignified, industrious, self-reliant spiritual being into a dependent animal creature without his knowing it. There is no avoiding this damage to character under the Welfare State.**

Barry Goldwater in **Conscience of a Conservative**

WELFARE'S EFFECTS

One of the worst aspects of welfarism and the Welfare State, of the notion that welfare is some kind of "right," is its effect on the integrity and morality not only of the people on welfare but of our people as a whole. We now actually have second, third and fourth generation welfare recipients. In the 10 years from 1960 to 1970 — years of great prosperity and full employment — our population increased only 13 percent but the number of people on welfare increased 94 percent and the costs increased 200 percent. Many experts believe at least a part of this fantastic increase is due to an attitude that can be summed up in the phrase: "Why work when I can get welfare?" In the government's food stamp plan, for instance, it recently was discovered that these stamps are being used by college students, workers out on strike and even military personnel, to say nothing of youngsters living in "hippie communes." We ourselves had the experience of a lady ahead of us in the super-market check-out line paying for her order with food stamps and then, on leaving the store, getting into a late-model Thunderbird.

Not long ago, New York City was a bit shocked to discover that its welfare bureaucrats had housed a welfare family in the Waldorf-Astoria Hotel, though the city has been providing housing for some 5,000 welfare families in various hotels at rentals averaging $650 a month. But hardly anyone commented on the fact that the lady housed in the Waldorf complained about the service. She said the maid didn't make up the beds until around noon. This is what is meant by the effect of welfare on integrity and morality — evidently it never occurred to her, living on taxpayers' money at Waldorf rates, that she do as millions of tax-payers' wives do: make her own beds. On top of this came the revelation that a federal model cities program footed the bill for a New England ski weekend for 34 youths and six chaperons at $60 each. One of the welfare bureaucrats couldn't see any difference between sending the kids to a summer camp and sending them away in the winter. The summer camps cost far less. Skiing is not an inexpensive sport and, it was asked, how many taxpaying earners must deny it to their own kids for this very reason?

Such examples could be multiplied endlessly. Perhaps, as someone suggested, we'll never solve the welfare problem until we recapture the old adage that charity begins at home — and that it *is* charity, not a "right" to which anyone is entitled at the expense of everyone else.

FACT AND OPINION

This discussion exercise is designed to promote experimentation with one's ability to distinguish between fact and opinion. It is a fact, for example, that the United States has been militarily involved in the Vietnam War. But to say this involvement serves the interests of world peace is an opinion or conclusion. Future historians will agree that American soldiers fought in Vietnam, but their interpretations about the causes and consequences of the war will probably vary greatly.

Some of the following statements are taken from readings in this book and some have other origins. Consider each statement carefully. Mark (O) for any statement you feel is an opinion or interpretation of the facts. Mark (F) for any statement you believe is factual. Then discuss and compare your judgments with those of other class members.

O = OPINION
F = FACT

_____ 1. A society that possesses the means sufficient to satisfy the basic life-needs of all its citizens and does not do so is morally deficient.

_____ 2. Many people on welfare are just too lazy to work.

_____ 3. By and large, welfare support goes to those who genuinely need it.

_____ 4. The tragedy of welfare is that it takes away from people the drive to work.

_____ 5. The United States spends less of its Gross National Product on welfare programs than do most other industrial nations.

_____ 6. The United States is becoming more and more of a welfare state.

_____ 7. Our present welfare system needs a complete revision.

_____ 8. Much more should be done by our government to help the poor.

_____ 9. Most people are on welfare because of a lack of ambition and willingness to work.

_____10. Some people are on welfare because they receive more money on welfare than they would by working.

_____11. Government assistance in time of need is a right possessed by the poor.

WHY MUST TAXPAYERS SUBSIDIZE IMMORALITY?

by Juanita Kidd Stout*

Juanita Kidd Stout, the first Negro woman to be elected judge in Pennsylvania, was born in Wewoka, Oklahoma. She is a graduate of the University of Iowa and took her master of laws degree and her doctorate in jurisprudence at Indiana University. She taught school, practiced law and, in 1959 was elected to the Philadelphia County Court for a ten-year term. Judge Stout is active in various civic organizations and writes and lectures extensively on the problems of dependent and delinquent children in the United States.

These questions may help your understanding of the reading:

1. What faults does the author find with our present welfare system?
2. What recommendations does Judge Stout make for the handling of children from the unfit home of a welfare recipient?
3. What other suggestions does Judge Stout have to improve our welfare system?

---

*Juanita Kidd Stout, *Why Must the Taxpayers Subsidize Immorality?* **The Philadelphia Sunday Bulletin**, March 7, 1965. Reprinted by permission of **The Philadelphia Evening** and **Sunday Bulletin**.

29

During the years I have been a judge in the Philadelphia County Court, I have learned a great deal about people on relief and about the people who hand out their checks. Frequently I have been outraged by both.

Last year there appeared before our court a child of 13 years who shortly was to be delivered of a baby fathered by her uncle. For at least ten years her family had been on relief — with a succession of men fathering a succession of children. The girl's 14-year-old sister had produced an illegitimate baby at 13; another older sister had borne an illegitimate child at 14.

But nothing had been done by welfare workers to take these girls, their brothers and sisters from their depraved home. In fact, one caseworker had filed a written report with the court stating that the mother was providing a "fairly adequate home" for her seven children.

On another occasion, a young man was brought before me on a charge of not supporting the child he had sired out of wedlock — nor was he contributing anything to the support of his own wife's five children. He had not held a steady job in ten years and had been on and off the relief rolls. I asked his caseworker if anyone had insisted that this healthy man find work. The answer was, "It is not our job to insist."

I said, "This man has completed 11th grade. He is neither stupid nor incapacitated. In the last ten years a great deal of grass has grown, a good many snows have fallen. Has no one directed him to a lawn mower, a snow shovel?"

The caseworker said no.

I then told the young man that if he failed to get a job in two weeks, or to prove that he had tried to get work by visiting 25 places of potential employment, he was going to jail. Four days later he reported back. He had a job.

In another case, a man brought before my court on the charge of failing to support three illegitimate children told me he had been "permitted" by a relief worker to set up a household with another woman. I didn't believe him, but investigation proved he was telling the truth.

The man was a part-time chauffeur and a partial relief recipient. Both women involved were receiving grants. When I called on the caseworkers of the man's two paramours for testimony, I learned that they indeed had knowledge of the situation. Not only that, but a supplementary grant had been approved for paramour No. 2, reimbursing her for $45 in "household money" she had used as bail to retrieve her lover from behind bars.

This shocks my conscience — moral as well as financial.

"I think I could have coped with wine, women and song, but then they threw pensions, welfare and medicare at me . . ."

The tragedy of relief is that it takes away from people the drive to work. When a person is capable of earning only $45 a week, he may be all too willing to accept $45 from public assistance for doing nothing. I have the deepest sympathy for the good mother struggling to bring up her children on a welfare grant, and for the father who wants but cannot find work. But I deplore a system that regards the handing out of checks as its prime function, that subsidizes the lazy and immoral home with the taxpayer's dollar.

Teen-age boys have appeared before me on charges of delinquency, and I have asked them what their fathers did for a living. Their answer: "We get a check from the state."

I get a check from the government, too. But there is one big difference; I work for mine. Too many youngsters in welfare-supported families never learn the value, the joy, the necessity of work — seeing, as they do, their fathers lying in bed until ten in the morning, and hearing the family finances discussed only in terms of "waiting until the check comes in."

Many social workers contend that the purpose of welfare is to keep families together. In my opinion, a good institutional home would be far better for the growth and development of children than an unfit private home where a child sees promiscuity, crime and vice, where the welfare check is used for everything but the child's support.

It is my suggestion that we provide dormitory facilities for these pitiful children, especially in the urban areas where the need is most acute, and that the public-assistance law be amended to provide grants for the children's support during the period of dormitory living. There our deprived youngsters would get the benefit of the taxpayer's dollar. They could be supervised in their studies and recreation. From there they could attend local schools. Each would have a clean bed, a warm meal and a light to read by — things many of them have never known. In the end, such a plan probably would be less expensive than our present system — or lack of system.

Social workers object to institutional care "because youngsters need mother love." They should sit in court with me and hear, day after day, the stories of some of that love: no genuine affection, no supervision, no conversation — nothing but a succession of "boarder" men.

There might be less need for special facilities if more of those involved in administering relief programs were concerned with seeing that a child has a decent upbringing. Certainly, welfare workers have heavy caseloads. But no achievement of substance comes easily, and the result of the extra effort can be inspiring, especially when you are dealing with human lives.

A few years ago five young girls involved in the slashing of another youngster in school were brought before me on a charge of delinquency. Some were from homes supported by welfare grants. None had had any previous contacts with the court. I decided on an experiment: I made each write an essay on the meaning of being a lady; each was told she must volunteer 100 hours of work in a hospital, a library or a home for the aged. And each must make a proper skirt, not tight and short like those they had worn in court.

These girls did not only everything the court assigned — but more. They learned the joy of work and of doing for others. They kept coming back even after I had released them from probation, and continually asked me: "What can we do next, Judge Stout?" None has been in trouble since. Two are now married, two are still in school, and one is working.

What these girls needed was helpful direction. Why didn't they receive such aid from a welfare worker before they came before our court?

No child, no adult, can remain on probation in my court unless he learns to read and write. (In Philadelphia we have third- and fourth-generation illiterates on relief.) Moreover, I will not hear the case of any boy, any man, who appears before me with his shirttail out, his hair unkempt. Neatness makes an astounding difference, not only in appearance but in outlook.

Certainly, I have the great prod of a jail sentence to get men to look for work, women to care for their children, and youngsters to keep out of trouble. But those who administer the welfare programs have as great a prod — the check.

It seems to me that attendance at free adult schools, to learn to read and write, should be a prerequisite of getting welfare money. If I can demand that a man bring me a list of 25 places where he has applied for work — or proof that he has enrolled in a training program — before I pass sentence in nonsupport cases, I believe welfare departments also can and should insist that he actively seek employment. If I can make it a part of juvenile probation that every youngster in my court bring me a study record signed by his parents or guardians, and his school report cards, why cannot a caseworker check such things?

Much can be done by welfare workers to lift people from the welfare environment. For example, there is great need for women in service jobs today, not just in homes but also in hospitals, office buildings and plants. A program could be developed whereby the best mother in a block — or perhaps the two best — would take on the day care of the small children while the other mothers took training and got jobs. The baby-sitting mothers would be paid by the working mothers, and all would be functioning as a part of our society.

I know as well as any social worker that the deplorable homes in our urban centers are breeding and multiplying indolence, illegitimacy, disrespect for law. I know, too, that the collection of relief checks is becoming one of the big occupations in this country. I believe strongly that a moral atmosphere in the home should be a factor in determining eligibility for welfare. An immoral home should not be subsidized.

As Chairman of the Subcommittee On Fiscal Policy Of The Joint Ecomonic Committee, I want to share with you the findings of a major staff study based on data gathered by the General Accounting Office at my request. ... Our staff has been working away for over a year now, describing and analyzing the whole range of welfare programs. We counted up 100 programs, and found they cost federal taxpayers more than $100 billion a year. But we wanted to know more. We wanted to show welfare in practice, not just in theory. We asked the GAO:"Who's getting these benefits? How much are they getting in all, and from how many programs are they receiving it?'' ... If I had to give you the conclusions ... it would be the following: For years we have been designing programs as if each had its own unique constituency and as if each operated all by itself. We haven't paid much attention to coordinating them. We haven't added them all up. And what has happened? We've ended up with so many programs that they can't be run well. Some people are left out while others scoop up thousands — far more than we could possibly provide to everyone in similar circumstances on a fair basis. And no one is in charge of all this.

Remarks of Congresswoman Martha W. Griffiths at press conference announcing major welfare study, March 22, 1973.

THE CONSTITUTION
AND THE WELFARE STATE

by Hubert H. Humphrey*

Mr. Humphrey, a native of South Dakota, is currently a United States Senator from Minnesota. He was Vice President of the United States from 1965 until 1969 and early in his career he served as mayor of Minneapolis. He is also an educator and the author of several books.

Reflect on the following questions while you read:

1. How does Senator Humphrey point out that the U.S. Constitution supports the idea of the welfare state?
2. Why does Senator Humphrey feel that more Americans need economic assistance today than our forefathers 150 years ago?
3. After reading Senator Humphrey's statement, why might you label him a liberal?

*Hubert H. Humphrey, *The Welfare State — A State of the General Welfare*, **The Social Welfare Forum**, 1950. National Conference of Social Work. New York: Columbia University Press, 1950, pp. 55-61. Reprinted by permission of Columbia University Press.

Those of us who associate ourselves with the liberal tradition in American politics are striving for an expansion of democratic life in the United States. We are trying to achieve a more perfect democracy in which the people through their government — the instrument they have created for working together — can build a constantly improving society. Our program is one for political democracy.

Those who would criticize our principles accuse us of creating a welfare state. They raise the cry of socialism. In my opinion, the use of these slogans is an attempt to confuse the issues and to escape facing those issues. Intelligent political participation calls for us to raise the level of political discussion so that the issues rather than the slogans are discussed. . . .

The welfare state has been an American objective ever since the Constitution was adopted a hundred and fifty years ago. We will recall that the Constitution charged the government with the responsibility to provide for the "general welfare" of the people. A state which is devoted to the welfare of its members, a state which works upon man and his welfare as an end in itself, is one I support, is one that is perfectly consistent with American traditions, and is one which I urge you to support. . . .

For the first time in the world's history we have an opportunity to establish a society in which every family can have a decent standard of living and in which luxury living will be available for many. It can be a society in which all have enough without unduly limiting the rewards available for the more industrious and the more able. . . .

Just as our industrial society has created for us greater wealth, it has also created for us complexities which have frequently limited the availability of that wealth to vast numbers of American people. It submerged man by steel and cement cities, by thousand-acre factories, by ten-thousand-acre farms, and by the paper corporations that control them. In the society of 150 years ago with our country new and our people few in number the need for economic freedom was not so important as it is today. There were vast rich resources crying for development. Economic opportunity was open to all.

Today, however, millions of families are dependent on jobs that may disappear tomorrow through no fault of their own. Millions of families, as social workers so well know, barely eke out bare subsistence as they live on tiny, worn-out farms which cannot produce decent livings even with the most industrious care. . . .

The vital program of American liberalism calls for a large number of reforms, of important, even basic changes on the face of our American society. There is nothing to fear in change. The very essence of growth calls for slow but steady change. Our faith in change is nothing more than the expression of our faith that man himself is going upward and that man and society can move ahead.

THE DIALOGUE

We have already moved far. We have seen men and women in this nation assemble in cooperative, free effort to improve their homes, their communities, their regions, and their nations. They have done so in cooperative effort with their government. They have used their government as their servant. They have recognized as Abraham Lincoln did in 1854 that "the purpose of government is to do for the people what they cannot do for themselves." They welcomed, even at the very beginning of the founding of our republic, assistance for education; for wagon roads so that everyone, not only the rich, could travel easily; for canals and levees; for public buildings; for railroads. A total of 250 million acres of land was granted by our government during those early days for various "welfare propositions." . . .

The philosophy of the welfare state aims to satisfy at least four major objectives:

1. A comprehensive social insurance program including insurance and provisions against the hazards of old age, disability, unemployment, and costs of medical care. The giant social security system is a striking example of cooperation on a national scale to do for ourselves together what we each cannot do alone.

2. Prevention or mitigation of unemployment through public works planning and monetary and fiscal policies

3. Improvement of the standard of living through such programs as slum clearance and public housing and by providing better facilities and opportunities for education

4. Limitations on the growth of powerful corporate enterprise with a view to protecting the interests of small business firms and less privileged elements within our society. . . .

The issue of the welfare state brings a vision to my mind. This vision symbolizes the choice which the American people face. On the one hand are those who would judge America and its accomplishments in terms of balance sheets and accounting records. On the other hand are those who judge America by its concrete accomplishments and by the happiness of its people. Those who oppose the welfare state remind me of the frightened men totting up their balances while the American people continue to go forward, building dams and houses and electric and telephone lines. . . .

38

If our political opponents wish to label the program we stand for as a "welfare state," then let it be so. Call it what you will, one fact, however, stands out in bold relief. This program has raised the living standards of American people. It has given a modicum of security to all areas of our population. It has provided a floor on living standards. It is furnishing relief from the apprehensions and anxieties which lead men to surrender their freedom. It is providing minimum protection against the hazards of old age and unemployment. It will provide prevention from catastrophe of sickness and disease. It is giving decent shelter to more and more of our people. It is putting a floor under wages. It will provide federal aid to education so as to give every boy and girl equal educational opportunities so that none will remain the slaves of ignorance.

These programs are strengthening the ring of freedom that centuries of struggle has drawn around Western man. These programs are providing the incentive and will set the example which will undermine totalitarianism wherever it may be.

DISTINGUISHING BETWEEN STATEMENTS THAT ARE PROVABLE AND THOSE THAT ARE NOT

From various sources of information we are constantly confronted with statements and generalizations about social problems. In order to think clearly about these problems, it is useful if one can make a basic distinction between statements for which evidence can be found, and other statements which cannot be verified because evidence is not available, or the issue is so controversial that it cannot be definitely proved. Students should constantly be aware that social studies texts and other information often contain statements of a controversial nature. The following exercise is designed to allow you to experiment with statements that are provable and those that are not.

In each of the following questions indicate whether you believe it is provable (P), too controversial to be proved to everyone's satisfaction (C), or unprovable because of the lack of evidence (U).

P = PROVABLE
C = TOO CONTROVERSIAL
U = UNPROVABLE

_____ 1. The federal government is the most efficient dispenser of welfare funds and sevices.

_____ 2. Only a small minority of welfare recipients are undeserving of assistance and able to work.

_____ 3. An expanded welfare system would be too expensive and too much of a burden on the taxpayers.

_____ 4. It is impossible to properly police and eliminate abuses in a national welfare program run by the federal government.

_____ 5. An expanded welfare system would make our society more susceptible to communism.

_____ 6. Expanded welfare states, such as in Sweden and Great Britain, have been failures.

_____ 7. Living on welfare can do psychological harm to a recipient.

_____ 8. Poverty could be eliminated within the next fifty years.

_____ 9. The U.S. Constitution justifies the extension of the welfare state.

WHAT PRICE THE
WELFARE STATE?

by Dr. Ruth Alexander*

> Dr. Ruth Alexander, a lecturer and columnist, pre-
> sented this address at the 56th Congress of American
> Industry, sponsored by the National Association of
> Manufacturers, in New York City on December 6, 1951.

As you read try to answer the following questions:

1. What does the author see as the primary consequence
   of the welfare state?
2. How does Dr. Alexander see the welfare state as being
   opposed to constitutional government?
3. Why does the authoress claim that "poverty is the best
   policy" under the welfare state?

*Dr. Ruth Alexander. *What Price the Welfare State?* **Vital Speeches**,
January 15, 1952, pp-199-203. Reprinted by permission of **Vital
Speeches.**

The common denominator of all Welfare States, which vary in degree but not in kind, is that the seat of authority is vested in the State — not in the citizens. It is not government OF or BY the people but OVER the people. The State is the Master, and THE people become ITS people — subjects of all-powerful, self-perpetuating government. Voting may continue but is reduced to a mere formality, as political favoritism progressively determines the outcome of elections.

In its early stages, the Welfare State governs by 'emergency decrees.' But gradually, as emergencies occur again and again, they reveal themselves to have been designed for keeps. Their purpose was to transfer power from the people to the State. For socialism regards revolution as a means to the end — POWER. Its cynical humanitarianism that "the end justifies the means" implies that it is based on an heroic redress of economic wrongs. But social gains are incidental. . . .

A primary consequence of the Welfare State is, therefore, Executive Government. Government by a Man — or Men. Not government by Law. It does not exist to serve the general welfare but to serve the welfare of special interests in return for political support. It obstructs the general welfare on behalf of these selective groups by its planned economy, especially by its managed money. Labor and the farmers, called in Europe Workers and Peasants, and those who are unable or unwilling to produce what they must, of necessity, consume, are the beneficiaries of Welfare State economy.

In the United States, organized labor has been given preferential treatment in the courts and has been absolved from anti-trust laws. In cases where the escalator clause was part of the wage agreement, labor was further provided with a hedge against inflation. This resulted in an unfair advantage over management, but it assured labor's political support. Similarly, the farmers were guaranteed relative immunity from inflation by the device of parity prices. Thus a favorable farm vote was also assured.

Constitutional government, on the other hand, exists to promote the general welfare, as enjoined by the Founders of this Republic. It is government by law — not men — and rests on the greatest good to the greatest number. To economic Man, this means the greatest quantity and the highest quality of goods and services at the lowest price to the greatest number. To political Man, it means the highest degree of freedom compatible with organized society. To

43

spiritual Man, it means the quality of mercy between man and his brother-man — a quality that is inconceivable between the remote impersonal State and the victims of its mass charity. Our Golden Rule declares that we must share one another's burdens on a voluntary basis. But it does not demand compulsory charity on a conveyor-belt basis. We all recognize that the mentally and physically sick and the helpless aged must be cared for by their neighbors, if they or their families are unable or unwilling to care for them. But we can, and always have, cared for them at local levels where human distress could not be exploited for political purposes. Under the 'Welfare' State, misery is for sale and the price is a vote. . . .

In short, constitutional government aims at progressive extension of individual liberty as the sole basis for human happiness. It is the real revolutionary, the true progressive, opposed to the retrogressive Welfare State that would take us backward down the long dark road from freedom to bondage — bondage to the so-called 'social whole.'

The economic outline of the Welfare State is as follows. If you work hard and save part of what you earn, you will have to support others. If you don't, they will have to support you. The inescapable conclusion is, therefore, that POVERTY IS THE BEST POLICY. . . .

Universal equality of goods and services, is the avowed aim of the Welfare State. Those at the bottom know they cannot reach the top. So they delight in bringing the top down to their level.

The Welfare State subscribes to this primitive and perverted interpretation of equality instead of equality before law. It reverses the role of privilege. Under its aegis, those who produce and exchange our goods and services are the underprivileged classes. They are helpless before the progressive plunder of their earnings and their savings by the State. . . .

In contrast to the harassed and underprivileged creators of our national wealth, are the beneficiaries of the Welfare State. They are the newly privileged classes. Like the aristocrats of old, these modern Princes of Privilege can enforce their demands that others support them. Nobody knows whether their dependent status was brought about through misfortune, evil doing, or intent. And nobody cares — as long as they deliver the votes.

WELFARE WONDERLAND

SELF-RELIANCE

ROAD OF LIFE

DEMORALIZATION

WELFARE

WELFARE CHECK

BY BELVA DETLOF

HB

As time goes on, they claim a right to everything for which they feel a need or which they see their neighbors enjoy. Content to begin at subsistence level, social workers soon make them discontent. Food, clothing and shelter is soon discarded for demands for kinds of each. Quality, not quantity, becomes their cry, as they are excited by professional reformers who tell them that their lot is undeserved; that it is somebody else's fault; that society 'owes' them a living. What they owe to society is conveniently omitted. And nobody reminds these Welfare beneficiaries that the price of privilege is slavery.

Constitutional government is limited to guaranteeing every citizen the right to pursue happiness. But Welfare government guarantees the possession of happiness as well, in return for political support. . . .

Capitalism has done more to eradicate poverty by the simple system of rewarding success and punishing failure, than any other system known to Mankind. Capitalism inherited poverty from its predecessor, the Welfare State of feudal socialism. It did not 'create' poverty. On the contrary, CAPITALISM CREATED WEALTH. It is the great Humanitarian of History for it freed man from bench labor — it gave him leisure and translated the luxuries of former days into the necessities of today. . . .

In short, the Welfare State kills political freedom and economic incentive. It begins slowly by controlling things. It ends by controlling US. It begins by proclaiming Government as our Guardian. It ends by establishing Government as our Master. It begins by 'protecting' MEN. It ends by destroying MAN.

FREEDOM AND THE
GENERAL WELFARE

by Senator Herbert H. Lehman*

This reading was originally presented as an address by Senator Lehman of New York, at the 45th Anniversary Conference of the League for Industrial Democracy on April 15, 1950. At the conference, the League presented a citation to Senator Lehman for being "an outstanding leader in the battle for racial and religious equality and economic and social welfare here and abroad."

Bring the following questions to your reading:

1. What does Senator Lehman feel is the essential and basic program of the welfare state?
2. Why does the author feel that the welfare state is a good defense against totalitarianism?
3. Why does the author see insecurity as a greater danger to our economic system than communism?

*Herbert H. Lehman, *Freedom and the General Welfare*, **Freedom and the Welfare State** (New York: League for Industrial Democracy, 1950), pp. 8-11. Reprinted with permission from the League for Industrial Democracy.

ALARMISTS AND WELFARE LEGISLATION

It has become fashionable in circles of political reaction to attack the concept of the welfare state as being prejudicial to individual liberty and freedom. These reactionaries view with fright and alarm the current and proposed activities of government in the fields of housing, health, and social security.

"These are steps on the road to Communism", the alarmists cry. But these same men uttered the same cries in the same tones of fear and outrage when President Roosevelt proposed the Securities and Exchange Act, the Fair Labor Standards Act, the Holding Company Act, the Federal Deposit Insurance Act and many other pieces of legislation which even reactionaries would not dare to attack today. The same cries were raised when Woodrow Wilson proposed the Federal Trade Commission Act in 1913 and when the Railway Labor Act was first placed on the statute books in 1926. I could cite laws and programs by the score enacted over the violent opposition of the reactionaries — laws and programs which were assailed as communistic at the time — but which are now accepted even in the most conservative circles.

This cry of state tyranny has been raised during the last half century whenever the community has attempted to interfere with the right of a few to destroy forests, exploit little children, operate unsanitary and unsafe shops, indulge in racial or religious discrimination, and pursue other policies endangering the health, safety and welfare of the community. These few have completely ignored the fact that, when their license to exploit the community was restricted, the freedom of the many from ignorance, insecurity, and want — the freedom of the many to live the good life — was measurably enhanced.

SOCIAL WELFARE VS. SPECIAL PRIVILEGE

I do not believe that our Federal government should seek to assume functions which properly belong to the individual or to the family, to the local community, or to free organizations of individuals. But I do believe that our Federal government should and must perform those functions which, in this complex and interdependent society, the individual, the family, or the community cannot practicably perform for themselves.

Today we in America and in the entire freedom-loving world are confronted with a world-wide threat to that principle which we hold most dear, the principle of individual dignity and of individual freedom. For the preservation of that principle we are willing to dedicate our lives, if it should prove necessary. But while this is a threat which we face on the world front, we face another danger here at home. That is the threat to our freedom from those within our country who would identify individual freedom with special privilege. Any move to diminish privilege, to stamp out discrimination and to bring security to our citizens is branded by these people as un-American.

Not so long ago an American political leader said that "the governments of the past could fairly be characterized as devices for maintaining in perpetuity the place and position of certain privileged classes. The government of the United States, on the other hand, is a device for maintaining in perpetuity the rights of the people, with the ultimate extinction of all privileged classes." Was it some Communist, some irresponsible radical or reformer, who made that statement? No, it was not. It was the late President Calvin Coolidge in a speech at Philadelphia in 1924.

It is my firm belief that the extinction of special privilege is an essential and basic program of the welfare state. Today the forces of special privilege provide the chief opposition and raise the wildest cries of alarm against economic security for all.

WELFARE STATE A FOE OF TOTALITARIANISM

In addition to the forces of special privilege who are opposed, on principle, to all social legislation, there are some who, while paying lip service to liberalism, claim to be troubled by the expanding scope of government in its direct concern with the welfare of the individual citizen. These people, while conceding merit to the specific programs of the welfare state, and while approving the welfare state programs of the past, join with the forces of privilege in contending that if the government provides any further services, it is moving in the direction of totalitarianism.

In my opinion these men of little vision have lost sight of the most important — and to me the most obvious — truth of our times — that a government which has secured the greatest degree of welfare for its people is the government which stands most firmly against totalitarianism. The critics of the welfare state do not understand this simple fact. They spend their time looking for Communists in and out of government and at the same time attack those measures which would deprive Communists and would-be Communists of their ammunition — and of their audience. The measures which would provide for the welfare of the people are the surest weapons against totalitarianism.

The Communist international, its leaders, and their philosophy, have been responsible for many designs which we in the democratic world consider the quintessence of evil. Certainly the suppression of basic rights — the police state and the slave labor camp — constitutes the most repulsive and obnoxious way of life we can imagine.

But, as a liberal, I have a *special* resentment against the Communists. I feel that one of their greatest disservices to the cause of human progress has been their identification of economic security with the suppression of freedom. It is their claim that in order to achieve the solution of the economic needs of the many, it is necessary to curb the freedoms of all. They say, in effect, that you cannot have a full stomach and a free mind at the same time.

I reject this concept! I reject it as being the ultimate in reaction. This is but another demonstration of the basic affinity between Communists and reactionaries in their thinking about man and his problems. *Both* groups believe that a nation of free men cannot possibly conquer the scourges of hunger, disease, lack of shelter, intolerance and ignorance. And they *both* have much to gain if they convince enough people that freedom and security are incompatible.

INSECURITY A THREAT TO FREEDOM

It is a strange paradox that the same conservatives and reactionaries who pose as champions of national security express the greatest antagonism toward individual security. Most of us readily acknowledge that the nations of the world cannot be free if they are not secure. It seems equally logical to me that *individuals* cannot be free if they are beset by fear and insecurity. To my mind the welfare state is simply a state in which people are free to develop their individual capacities, to receive just awards for their talents and to engage in the pursuit of happiness, unburdened by fear of actual hunger, actual homelessness or oppression by reason of race, creed or color.

The fear of old age, the fear of sickness, the fear of unemployment, and the fear of homelessness are not — as some would have us believe — essential drives in a productive society. These fears are not necessary to make free competitive enterprise work. The fear of insecurity is rather a cancer upon free competitive enterprise. It is the greatest threat which confronts our economic system. I hasten to add that I believe in free competitive enterprise. I believe it is the best system yet devised by man. But it is not a goal in itself. It must always serve the public interest.

We have had twenty years of the New Deal and the Fair Deal. Who would say that the American worker, the American farmer and the ordinary American businessman is less free than he was twenty years ago? Actually, freedom in the true sense flourishes more generally and more widely today than ever before in our history. The worker, the farmer and the businessman have vastly more freedom than they ever had before. They are freer to enjoy the fruits and benefits of a productive economy and a full life. But they are not yet free enough.

We are still far from the goal we seek. Insecurity still haunts millions. Inadequate housing poisons the wells of family life in vast numbers of cases. Inadequate schooling handicaps a great segment of our people. And the fear of sickness and old age still clutches at the hearts of many if not most of our fellow citizens. Until we solve all these problems and quiet all these fears, our people will not be truly free.

BIAS & REASON

One of the most important critical thinking skills is the ability to distinguish between opinions based on emotions or bias and conclusions based on a rational consideration of facts. This discussion exercise is designed to promote experimentation with one's capacity to recognize biased statements.

The following statements have been taken from various readings in this book. Consider each statement carefully. Mark (R) for any statement you feel is based on a rational consideration of the facts. Mark (P) for any statement you believe is based on prejudice or emotion. Mark (I) for any statement you think is impossible to judge. Then discuss and compare your judgments with other class members.

R = REASON
P = PREJUDICE
I = IMPOSSIBLE TO JUDGE

_____ 1. By and large, welfare support goes to those who genuinely need it.

_____ 2. One of the worst aspects of welfarism and the Welfare State, or the notion that welfare is some kind of "right," is its effect on the integrity and morality not only of the people on welfare but of our people as a whole.

_____ 3. The common denominator of all Welfare States, which vary in degree but not in kind, is that the seat of authority is vested in the State — not in the citizens.

_____ 4. A government which has secured the greatest degree of welfare for its people is the government which stands most firmly against totalitarianism.

_____ 5. Naturally people like getting something for nothing and will reward the politician who votes for larger doles by returning him to office again and again.

_____ 6. In reality, the WPA was a highly effective weapon in damping down the social and economic holocaust of the Great Depression.

_____ 7. Hard work is the answer to the welfare problem.

_____ 8. The level of welfare payments in every state in the union is nothing but guaranteed annual poverty.

_____ 9. Under the Welfare State, the earnings of the more productive and efficient individuals are tapped for the benefit of the less productive and less efficient.

THE VANISHING REPUBLIC

by Jack McGann*

> Jack McGann is a legislative aide for Liberty Lobby, which describes itself as "a pressure group for patriotism — the only lobby registered with Congress which is wholly dedicated to the advancement of governmental policies based on our Constitution and Conservative principles." This reading is an excerpt from a statement presented by Mr. McGann before the Senate Finance Committee on August 26, 1970.

The following questions should help you examine the reading:

1. Why did our founding fathers, in Mr. McGann's opinion, establish a republic rather than a direct democracy?
2. How does the author define such terms as socialism, communism and Americanism?
3. What lesson does Uruguay recommend to those who favor the welfare state, in the author's estimation?

---

*This reading was presented as a statement by Jack McGann for Liberty Lobby before the Senate Finance Committee on the *Family Assistance Plan*. The statement is reprinted with the permission of Liberty Lobby.

VANISHING REPUBLIC

More than 200 years ago, Prof. Alexander Tyler mused that:

> A democracy cannot exist as a permanent form of government. It can only exist until the voters discover that they can vote themselves largess from the public treasury. From that moment on, the majority always votes for the candidate promising the most benefits from the public treasury, with the result that a democracy always collapses over loose fiscal policy . . . always followed by a dictatorship.

To many, socialism sounds like a conservative scare word without much basis in fact. But by what other name can you refer to a transitional society which increasingly "takes from each according to his ability and renders to each according to his need." The unvarnished truth of this new welfarism concept being espoused by the Administration is a plan which takes a sharp turn toward this socialist principle.

Our founding fathers realized that a democracy was a poor form of government and that is why they established a republic. "Let the people's will be done," cries the politician. Naturally people like getting something for nothing and will reward the politician who votes for larger doles by returning him to office again and again. No wonder a skeptic was heard to remark that "if a politician tries to buy votes with private money, he's a crook; but if he tries to buy them with the people's money, he's a great liberal."

The unhappy fact of this parasitic welfare plan is that as more and more are receiving public money, fewer and fewer will be providing it until diminishing returns set in and we become a classless society. Conditions have reached such calamitous proportions that it now seems that if you want your father to take care of you, that's paternalism; if you want your mother to take care of you, that's maternalism; if you want Uncle Sam to take care of you, that's socialism; if you want your comrades to take care of you, that's communism; but if you want to take care of yourself, that's Americanism!

DIGNITY MUST BE EARNED

Repeatedly, . . . we hear the vociferous demands of the welfare rights groups complaining that they need addi-

tional relief so as to be able to live in dignity. Hear what Dr. Thomas Mathew, noted Negro neurosurgeon, says on that score: "Dignity can only be earned . . . Our grandparents had a guaranteed income — they called it slavery."

For a man to be totally free, he must have some measure of independence, and handouts from the government only exacerbate his dependency, and correspondingly reduce his freedom. The theory of welfarism is that people prefer security to freedom; each advance of the welfare state takes with it another slice of individual liberty. As generations pass along, this concept of absolute right of guaranteed income becomes increasingly more difficult to turn back. As Churchill said, "You cannot unscramble an egg."

If we choose to permit socialism to gain control of our country, let us be prepared to accept the baleful consequences, amply illustrated in Britain as the professional "brain-drain" continues. Let us also look southward to Uruguay, a country which has more doctors per capita than the U.S. Henry Hazlitt observes in his book Man Vs. the Welfare State:

> Uruguay's warning to the U.S. and to the world is that governmental welfarism, with its ever-increasing army of pensioners and other beneficiaries, is fatally easy to launch and fatally easy to extend, but almost impossible to bring to a halt — and quite impossible politically to reverse, no matter how obvious and catastrophic its consequences become. . . .

WHY NOT ANOTHER WPA?

by Cabell Phillips*

Mr. Phillips worked for the WPA and the NYA in the thirties, has been on the Washington staff of the New York Times for over a quarter of a century, and is writing a political and social history of the forties.

Use the following questions to assist you in your reading:

1. Why did President Roosevelt feel that "the dole" was a poor way to combat poverty and unemployment?
2. Why does the author recommend government work projects over direct relief payments?

*Cabell Phillips, *Why Not Another WPA?* **The New Republic**, February 6, 1971, pp. 19-20. Reprinted by permission of **The New Republic** © 1971, Harrison-Blaine of New Jersey, Inc.

To most people under forty the WPA (it stand for Works Progress Administration) is something they came across in a textbook. And to many — maybe most — of those over forty it evokes a cluttered mental montage of Harry Hopkins, "boondoggles," political corruption, and a lazy bum leaning on his shovel while drawing government pay.

In reality, the WPA (along with such kindred agencies as the National Youth Administration and the Civilian Conservation Corps) was a highly effective weapon in damping down the social and economic holocaust of the Great Depression. It did not "cure" the depression — it took a world war to do that — but it profoundly eased the depression's cruel impact upon millions of families and it helped greatly, maybe decisively, to stabilize a severely shaken social structure. Ten to twelve million jobless men — that was the score in 1932-1935 — with their families sunk for a year or more to varying depths of suffering and hopelessness can shake a social structure pretty severely. Then, as now, there were marches, demonstrations and bloody confrontations with the cops.

The Hoover Administration had refused as a matter of principle and morality to do anything directly to alleviate unemployment and its attendant destitution. Early in the tempestuous "hundred days" of the New Deal, President Roosevelt set up the Federal Emergency Relief Administration, and in the next year and a half funneled nearly a billion dollars out to the states (it wasn't called revenue-sharing then), but most of it to be used simply as a dole to feed the hungry and house the homeless.

Hopkins argued, and the President in time agreed, that the dole was a dead-end. It was destructive of human dignity and enterprise and yielded no returns to the state. The way to fight unemployment, he said, was with jobs where a man (or woman) could earn his keep in the time-honored way by honest toil. The formula was work relief instead of direct relief.

The WPA was launched early in 1935, its bureaucratic fingers reaching into every city and county in the nation. By the end of 1940 it had spent over $10-billion, 80 percent of it in wages scaled approximately at prevailing rates: they averaged out to between $50 and $60 a month. (Believe it or not, that was, just barely, a "living wage.") These wages went to an average of 2.1 million otherwise jobless persons during each of those years, reaching a peak of 3.5 million late in 1938. Altogether, some 8 million individuals —

equivalent to one-fifth of the nation's labor force — worked on WPA projects at some time or other between 1935 and the end of 1940.

What kind of work?

For a comprehensive look at social security programs in various countries, see the publication, **Social Security Programs Throughout the World**, 1971, by the U.S. Department of Health, Education, and Welfare. This 249 page book is available from the Superintendent of Documents, United States Government Printing Office, Washington, D.C. 20402, for $2.25. Refer to this number when ordering: DHEW Publication No. (SSA) 72-11802.

Most of the thousands of projects were devised locally. They covered just about every field of human endeavor and public need: roads, streets and sewers; parks, playgrounds and levees for flood control; repair and building of schools, jails and libraries. WPA white-collar workers taught thousands of illiterates to read and write, manned hundreds of public health centers and home nursing services, refurbished invaluable land- and tax-records from ancient courthouse basements, organized symphony orchestras, and theatrical companies of at least passable professional caliber, wrote and published the incomparable American Guide Series in some thirty-odd volumes. Et cetera.

Let it be said that they also sometimes raked nonexistent leaves, built roads to nowhere, exhaustively researched the history of the safety pin and otherwise gave substance to the term, "boondoggle." And sure enough, politics reared its ugly head here and there in their midst. Reporter Thomas L. Stokes won a Pulitzer in 1939 for his expose of how the Democrats "bought" an election in Kentucky "with WPA money."

This is what seems so easy to remember about WPA. But one's catalogue should also include such durable monuments as New York's LaGuardia Airport and Jones Beach, which got their starts as WPA projects — as did Chicago's handsome lakefront park, St. Louis's impressive riverfront development, and the municipal recreation center in San Francisco's Aquatic Park. There are thousands of lesser monuments scattered across the land whose inscriptions have faded. No one ever claimed for WPA that it was the most efficient method of performing public works. Even so, the material return on the investment was substantial: things that urgently needed doing were done.

But WPA's big payoff was in the salvage of human values; in preserving the work skills, the pride and the initiative of millions whose faith in the democratic process had worn dangerously thin. And that is at the heart of the dilemma facing President Nixon today. His problem is not greatly different from Roosevelt's. Billions of dollars are going down the welfare drain with scarcely visible returns, either in material or human terms. At the same time that people who can, and for the most part want to, work are swelling the relief rolls by thousands each week, local governments are curtailing essential services because they are too broke to hire the people to carry them on.

Skills, morale and faith in the democratic verities are going down the drain, too. "Made work," as WPA jobs used to be called, is not the optimum solution to such a wastage. But name a better substitute until that happy day of "a full-employment economy" comes along.

ABILITY TO EMPATHIZE

The ability to empathize, to see a problem from another person's vantage point, is a skill that must be widely developed and practiced if national problems, like public welfare assistance, are ever to be solved.

The Medical Committee for Human Rights* suggests the following general principles to underlie a plan for a government sponsored national health program:

General Principles for a National Health Plan

1. Health care must not be bought and sold like a commodity, but must truly become an individual and inalienable right. In order to do this, the transfer of money must be totally eliminated from the process of obtaining health care.

2. Health care must be paid for by a national or regional financing mechanism guaranteeing universal free access to comprehensive medical care.

3. The taxes used to pay for health care should be collected progressively: those best able to pay — corporations, banks, insurance companies, wealthy individuals — should bear the main burden of financing the system.

---

*The Medical Committee for Human Rights, born in 1964 of the civil rights struggle, believes that "the failure of health care is a symptom of the broader crisis of dehumanization, racism and greed in American society." It also believes that health care is a human right. The above principles are reprinted by permission of The Medical Committee for Human Rights.

4. No one should be allowed to profit from the sickness, misery and death of others. Thus all profit-making institutions should be prohibited from obtaining payments through the national health plan.

5. Hospitals, clinics and all other health institutions should be controlled by those who use them as well as those who work in them. Thus health institutions in local areas should be planned and run by elected neighborhood councils. Representatives from the neighborhood health councils would sit on regional and national councils to coordinate the planning. All money collected through the financing mechanism must be paid to these community-worker controlled health councils.

6. Billions of dollars of the money collected should be allocated to build neighborhood-based community health centers, and to increase the numbers of all types of health workers. Each category of health manpower should include minority groups and women in proportion to their numbers in the population.

1. Try to empathize and imagine how each of the followng individuals or groups might react to the MCHR's suggested principles. Discuss and compare your reactions with other classmates.

2. Which two individuals or groups do you think would be the most sympathetic? Which two would be the most hostile? Why?

> A physician
> A welfare recipient
> The father of a large middle income family
> The father of a wealthy family
> An active member of Liberty Lobby
> A U.S. taxpayer
> An official of the National Welfare Rights
>   Organization

READING NUMBER 9

THE POVERTY PROFESSION

by the National Review*

The **National Review** is a weekly magazine edited by William F. Buckley, Jr. The following statement appeared as an editorial.

Consider the following questions while reading:

1. According to this editorial, what is different about being poor now as opposed to being poor in the past?
2. What is "the poverty game?"

The Poverty Profession*, **National Review, July 29, 1969, p. 739. Reprinted with the permission of **National Review** whose editorial offices are located at 150 East 35 Street, New York, N.Y. 10016.

In New York City, an activist group counsels welfare recipients on their rights: this family is entitled to a washing machine from "the city," that family, to a new couch for the living room. A woman in Appalachia praises the antipoverty worker who came to her town "and showed me how much I could get from all those government programs." A group of New York's largest stores has just extended credit privileges to welfare recipients. A construction worker in Connecticut reports that his union is trying to recruit young Negro apprentices but is having small luck because there is more money to be made on welfare. Poverty, it becomes daily clearer, is a legitimate and often permanent occupation, like steam-fitting or accountancy. As in other trades and professions, the more alert and energetic workers make the most money.

This goes against the traditional American grain. In the United States, where protestant capitalism triumphed as nowhere else, poverty was viewed as wrong, shameful, harmful to the poor person and to society. It mattered little where the blame was laid — on the indolent individual or on the stumbling economic system — the point was, it was bad to be poor and something had to be done about it. Now the question arises, what is *poor*? Today it is possible to be a professional povertyite and do rather nicely for oneself. "Poverty" has broken free of its two old connotations, want and disgrace: The smart povertyites no longer lack the essentials of life or even many of its luxuries; nor do they feel any guilt about their dependence upon society.

To keepers of the old faith, this is disturbing. Aroused, they cry out against "indolence," "subsidized illegitimacy," "sapping of initiative" et cetera. The tribunes of the poor respond by condemning objectors and objections as "callous," "heartless," "inhumane." The brouhaha is irrelevant; what is important is that professional poverty is here, and gives every sign of being here to stay.

Moreover, expectations tend to rise. As it becomes clear that one can do well in the poverty game, the welfare rolls grow; as one does well, one seeks to do better and so the cost-per-recipient rises as benefit after benefit is added to the list of things to which recipients feel themselves entitled. Fifty years ago, minimal food and shelter were judged enough; today the poverty professionals expect television sets, automobiles, credit at department stores, Easter wardrobes. As Milton Friedman put it, when you pay people to be poor, there are going to be plenty of poor people.

Not long ago, a European newspaper correspondent, interviewing residents of a Chicago slum, asked one teen-age girl what she wanted to do when she grew up.

"To draw," she replied.

The newsman, pleasantly surprised to find artistic interests in such unlikely surroundings, pursued his inquiry: "What kind of pictures do you like to draw?"

"Not pictures," replied the girl. "Drawing welfare like mother does."

George Champion, former chairman of the Board of Directors, Chase Manhattan Bank.

THE UPSIDEDOWN
WELFARE STATE

by Thomas H. Walz*

Thomas H. Walz is currently Dean of the School of Social Work, University of Iowa. He received his doctorate in social work from the University of Minnesota. He has served as director of the Peace Corp in Honduras. His book, **The Upsidedown Welfare State**, was published in 1973.

These questions should help you with your reading:

1. What does the author mean when he uses the terms "upsidedown welfare state" and "poorhouse state?"
2. What conflict does the author see between the upsidedown welfare state and the American concept of rugged individualism?
3. The reading points out three myths that Americans believe regarding welfare. What are they? Do you agree?

*Thomas H. Walz & Beth Zemek, **The Upsidedown Welfare State**, undated. This publication is a pamphlet commissioned by the Minnesota Resource Center for Social Work Education.

Upside-down welfarism is defined as the condition where those who need public aid the most, often receive the least; and where those who need public aid the least, often receive the most. The position taken is that welfare is upside-down only when the most helpless in the society are not accorded greatest public attention and support and when those most able to manage for themselves are given unnecessary public assistance.

The concept of the upside-down welfare state is to be credited to Michael Harrington, who ten years ago, noted that America was a society which provided "socialism for the rich and free enterprise for the poor."[1] To Harrington, there were really two Americas, one composed of the minority poor, and the other, composed of the majority non-poor middle and upper classes. He feared that the middle and upper income majority thru their control of the legislative process would pursue their own legislative self interests and would fail to deal justly and adequately with the minority poor. The data will show that there is much truth to Harrington's concern.

More recently another writer, Richard Elman, suggested that not only do we have upside-down welfare in this country but we have two separate systems of welfare to perpetuate it. He described the two systems as a "Poorhouse State" system which cares for the poor in highly visible, but meager ways and a "Welfare State" system which provides the middle and upper income groups with sizeable aid, but in carefully hidden ways.[2] There is considerable evidence to support this statement. . . .

THE WELFARE RECIPIENT

For many people, public welfare has come to mean programs which care for the poor and destitute thru some form of public aid dispensed by public agencies. To these people, welfare evokes a predictable set of images — welfare checks, food stamps, public high rises, and charity hospitals. Their image of welfare recipients generally consists of work-shy males, chronically ill aged, hungry children, mothers of illegitimate children and even occasionally of their purported boyfriends. Are these images real or are they figments of the burdened taxpayers imagination?

1. Michael Harrington, **The Other America** (Baltimore: Penquin Special, 1963), p. 157.

2. Richard Elman, **The Poorhouse State** (New York: Dell Publishing Company, 1966).

69

There are, of course, many poor in America, some 25 million more or less. Not all the poor, however, receive welfare in the form of public assistance. In fact, less than half do. But this is not the point of this publication. What should be of even greater importance to the taxpayer, is the extent to which the non-poor are recipients of public aid. If a more accurate definition of welfare was used, namely any program which used public monies to provide for the well being of individuals in the society, then nearly everyone could be considered on welfare. Our images of welfare and of the welfare recipient would necessarily have to be changed.

By using this new definition of welfare, it would be difficult to distinguish the $113,275 soil bank payment to Senator James Eastland of Mississippi from the $10.20 per month allowance provided an AFDC child in his state,[3] except in terms of the beneficence of the subsidy. Both are entitlements to public monies according to the laws of the land.

A review of almost any aspect of life — housing, transportation, education, health care — supports the contention that a great many persons in the society are being subsidized and assisted by tax dollars. The situation that has led us to view only the poor as "welfare recipients" is the high visibility of their aid (e.g., food stamps, welfare checks, high rises). Less visible are the many forms of public assistance diverted to the non-poor and even to the rich (e.g., tax breaks and write-offs, government contracts, consultantships, guaranteed loans, etc.)

The truth as to who is and who is not on welfare can only come through a careful analysis of the ofttimes wayward movements of the public's tax dollar. A sample of what one might expect to find is suggested by the following remarks of an Assistant Secretary of the Department of Housing and Urban Development, Floyd Hyde:

"Americans who pride themselves on being rugged individualists go through life attending public schools, receiving veterans benefits, financing homes with FHA mortgages, retiring on Social Security, or even receiving payments for not growing certain crops. But all these were regarded as public rights and they are somehow different from welfare payments which are regarded as handouts to the ungrateful poor . . . and if to the list we add those

3. Ronald Gelatt, ''The Politics of Hunger'', **Saturday Review**, June 21, 1969, p. 21.

people who hold FHA mortgages, receive farm subsidies, use Medicare, complete GI Bill financed education or receive investment credits on their taxes, or even work for companies with large government contracts, then we have few people who are not on welfare."[4]

> **The paradox of our society is that we have socialism for the rich and free enterprise for the poor.**

Michael Harrington

The fact that nearly everybody is on welfare should not be disturbing. What should be disturbing is the fact that most people think only the poor are on welfare, a view which is often accompanied by public attitudes of contempt and moral righteousness. Such attitudes are far from innocuous in that they create the climate within which welfare programs for the poor are administered. . . .

HISTORY OF WELFARISM

Upside-down welfarism is as American as apple pie. In effect it was set in motion by the Constitution of the United States. In Article I, Section VIII, the federal government was empowered to levy taxes and to provide for the general welfare. As history will show, the interpretation of the general welfare clause had a beneficial effect on an elite minority of the American people, but was not so generous to others. For nearly a century, blacks and other persons without property were largely neglected in most early measures of public welfare. Public assistance in general was greatly restricted by a political philosophy of laissez faire which considered major public aid to the poor by the Federal Government to be not only bad judgement, but unconstitutional.

4. **HUD NEWS**, U.S. Department of Housing and Urban Development, May 13, 1971, pp 4-5.

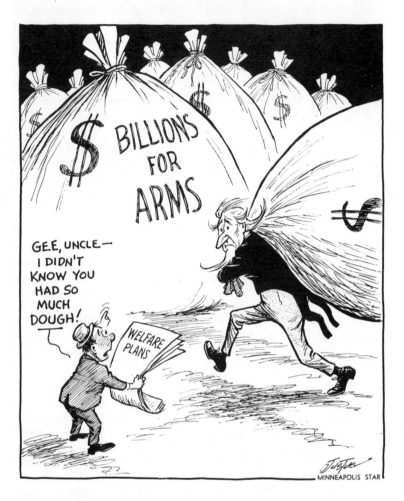

By the mid 1850's, however, the Federal government began one of the greatest public welfare programs of its early history — the giving away of public lands to the private sector. There were actually three such programs of land granting: a white man's land grant program (known as the Homestead Acts); a black man's land grant program (known as the Freedman's Acts), and the Railroad's land grant program. The first provided 160 acres, seed grain and a loan, available to anyone who had not borne arms against the government and who would undertake to cultivate it. The second offered 40 acres and a mule to former slaves, and the third provided millions of acres of prime public land to the giant private railroad industry. . . .

Other welfare measures were also granted in the mid 19th century. The Morril Act of 1862 subsidized agricultural education with public lands. At the same time access to the West was assured through continuing government subsidies of the railroads. In the ten years after the war, the country doubled its railroad mileage and the profits of construction and operation went to establish the fortunes of Vanderbilt, Gould, Huntington, Stanford and other multi-millionaires. [5]

Today who reaps the harvest of public subsidies? Have we seen a shift from the haves to the have nots or only from railroads to airlines? What follows is an updated analysis of the way todays public pie is being cut. . . .

HOUSING

A cursory review of Federal housing policies shows that our upside-down welfare pattern reappears in highly visible "warehouse" types of public housing projects for the poor. These programs frequently located the poor in dismal concentrations of misery unrelieved by adequate services and opportunities for escape. In contrast, the middle and upper income groups have enjoyed both substantial and discrete housing assistance. In housing, as in hunger, it is clear that the greatest need parallels the lowest incomes. As one writer (Elman) put it, the poorhouse state subsidizes the tenant while the welfare state subsidizes the landlord. . . .

The "welfare state" has subsidized at least partially over 30,000,000 units of housing for middle and upper income groups over the past 31 years through such programs such as FHA and GI financing. The "poorhouse state" during this same period has provided less than 800,000 units of low cost public housing for the poor. [6]

The "welfare state" through urban renewal has retrieved inner city land by tearing down old businesses and old neighborhoods with their low rent units and replacing them with new businesses and middle and upper income housing units. The "poorhouse state" has offered relocation services to the dispossessed poor, and only recently has made available some inadequately funded programs which allowed for rent and home purchase subsidies. [7] . . .

5. **Ibid.**, p. 805.
6. "How Public Spending Promotes Poverty" from the Kerner Commission Report.
7. Robert S. Benson and Harold Wolman Eds. **Counter Budget**, (New York: National Urban Coalition, 1971), p. 137.

JOHN WAYNE ON WELFARE ?

Actor John Wayne comes across to his admirers as a straight talking, straight shooting, rugged individualist. They must have been dismayed therefore, to learn that he is among those who have been crawling through loopholes to evade the government ceiling on farm subsidy payments.

Wayne and his partners in Arizona cotton land drew $810,000 in federal subsidies in 1970. The new law limiting each to a $55,000 per crop maximum federal subsidy check will reduce the payments to Wayne and his partners to $218,000. But more than $500,000 in additional subsidies will go to farmers and investors who leased land from Wayne and his group and paid them several hundred thousand dollars.

Wayne, whose stock in trade is cowboy and Indian movies, recently was asked how he viewed the demand by some Indians for 'reparation'. Wayne replied, 'I don't know why the government should give them something that it wouldn't give me . . . Years ago I didn't have all the opportunities either. But you can't whine and bellyache cause somebody else got a good break and you didn't, like these Indians are. We'll all be on a reservation soon if the socialists keep subsidizing groups like them with our tax money'.

Lo the Cowboy, **Minneapolis Tribune**, July 14, 1971.

TRANSPORTATION

Mobility is essential to modern life. It is as personally important for a senior citizen to get to a health clinic via public transportation as it is for a businessman to get from New York to Chicago on private transportation to close a business contract.

Federal policy has reacted unevenly to the transportation needs of its people. This is particularly evident with the expanding of suburbia, where the pressure built up rapidly for easy access and quick egress from urban centers. Endless acres of asphalt and concrete tangibly document government response to this public demand. Yet, with all the building of freeways, the remodeling of airports, and the millions invested in supersonic transportation, benign neglect continues to be the order of the day in respect to urban public transportation and mass transit relief from congested highways and streets.

These millions of dollars in federal transportation aids have contributed much to the general well-being and convenience of the trucking industry, the air traveler and the suburbanites, while those who live in the "poorhouse state" have been powerless to prevent the carving up of city neighborhoods for highways and the removal of industrial growth and development (which means jobs) to the suburbs. . . .

AGRICULTURE

The Agriculture Department, which next to the Defense Department is one of the fattest Federal bureaucracies, provides those farmers able to take advantage of it such public assistance as: CROP INSURANCE, PAYMENT FOR NOT PRODUCING CROPS, HOME LOANS, FARM LOANS, ASSISTANCE IN GRAIN STORAGE, EXTENSION PROGRAMS, ETC.

There are farmers who look like what we conventionally regard as farmers; there are farmers who look like corporations; and there are farmers who look like little more than human machines. Whom do you suspect public welfare in agriculture would be most apt to reach? The migrant worker; The tenant farmer; The small struggling farmer on his family farm; or the large corporate farmer?

The "welfare state" paid out in 1969 more than 3 billion in direct payments to growers for not producing such commodities as wheat, corn, cotton, etc. in the same year the "poorhouse state" allowed less than 20% of this amount for all of the various food distribution and food stamp programs established to aid the hungry poor.[8]

Programs which we have chosen to label "poorhouse state" programs regularly fall short of meeting the extent of need. Food stamps and USDA Commodity Distribution programs reach only 44% of those Americans too poor to escape hunger without public assistance and only 26% of the 24 million Americans living below the official poverty line.[9]

8. Federal Outlays Manual (F.O.M.), U.S. Department of Commerce, Washington, D.C., 1970.

9. **Op. Cit.**, Benson, p. 64.   75

The richest 10% of all farmers receive more than 50% of price support payments.[10]

In the Imperial Valley near the Hoover Dam, 550 large growers receive 12 million annually in farm subsidies, while 10,000 landless residents of the Valley exist on welfare payments totalling less than 8 million.[11] . . .

HEALTH CARE

One of the myths our society holds is that the United States affords its citizens the best health care in the world. This may be true of those whose incomes permit the purchase of top flight health care on the free market, but it is far from adequate in describing the quality of care provided the nation's poor. According to the President's Commission on Income Maintenance, the poor experience four times the amount of heart disease, six times the amount of nervous disorders, three times the number of orthopedic ailments, eight times the number of visual defects than the non-poor.

In addition, the poor suffered an infant mortality rate twice that of the non-poor; fifty per cent of the pregnant women who were poor received no prenatal care; fifty per cent of their children were not immunized properly; and 64 per cent had never seen a dentist.

Even the dramatic efforts to provide government health insurance (Medicare) has been drastically limited to all but a small portion of the population. It has yet to be extended to cover the young, even though the United States ranks number 13 among the industrial nations of the world in its infant mortality rate.[12] Despite all the platitudes about improvement in health care, the pattern of health care in the United States is still upside-down. We are the only industrial nation in the world not to offer its citizens comprehensive health insurance.

EDUCATION

There are only two principal roads to prosperity in the United States these days — inheritance and education. By inheritance even functional idiots could become million-

10.   P. Barnes, "Water for the Wealthy", **New Republic**, May 8, 1971, p.

11.   **Op. Cit.**, Benson, p. 197.

12.   **Op. Cit.**, Benson, p. 68.

aires. By education, especially with the help of subsidized higher education, many Americans can look forward to some measure of prosperity in their life time. Education, like health care, becomes one of the basic services required for achievement in a complex industrial society.

We would assume that a nation convinced of this critical role of education in the lives of its citizens and imbued with deep convictions about what is fair and just, would insure its people equal opportunity to quality education.

Instead we have vast inequities in school financing, physical plants, teaching and administrative ability, supportive services, psychological and career counseling, extracurricular and athletic opportunities. These variations run most deeply between inner city and suburban schools, with the most obvious disparity being school financing. The great American middle class dream is to live in a "nice neighborhood" with good schools. Good schools just go along with the nice neighborhood which goes along with affluence. We also know, without the aid of investigations or commissions, that the poor neighborhoods have less adequate schools. We sigh over how hard it is to bring up children in such neighborhoods because we see, accurately, that those inadequate schools are little but way stations on the bad trip to low paying jobs, the dreary "poorhouse state" cycle of poverty maintenance or prison. As long as school financing is tied to the economic status of the neighborhood or district, this is the way it will be. . . .

CONCLUSIONS

In this time of economic crises, it seems that more than ever before "No man is an island". It is more than just simply getting a job, if a man can find one, if he can work, if his skills are needed, if indeed he has any salable skills. If . . . . . The "ifs" are dependent upon the whole and the poor are dependent upon the affluent society which is part of that whole. John Kenneth Galbraith has said, "few things have been more productive of controversy over the ages than the suggestion that the rich should, by one device or another, share their wealth with those who are not. With comparatively rare and usually eccentric exceptions, the rich have been opposed to this." [13]

13. John Kenneth Galbraith, **The Affluent Society** (Boston: Houghton-Mifflin, 1963) p. 69.

We can no longer oppose that which is each man's birthright. Even engineers, executives, scientists and skilled craftsmen are finding that we can no longer expect each man to compete for economic security in an economically closed society. If we are to have a work ethic, reasonable and available work opportunities must be developed.

There are some basic myths that linger in our society to perpetuate our confusion about the concept of welfare. These myths tend to be more tenacious than reason in explaining and justifying the human condition, especially when deeply meaningful human values are involved. The three myths[14] about the nature of poverty are:

1. The myth of the economic whip, or the belief that the threat of starvation is the only real motivating force that keeps the shoulders of the masses to the economic wheel.

2. The myth of the superabundant work opportunities; the belief that anyone who really wants to work can find a job.

3. The bootstrap fantasy, the myth of the self-made man, or the belief that all men have the necessary resources, if they will only use them to compete in the market place. . . .

Now that we no longer see the welfare system only in terms of the people at the bottom of the economic heap, perhaps a new attitude can make possible a reshuffling of priorities. Each of us has a share in this upside-down welfare system and those at the top have the means at hand to abolish it.

14.   Paul E. Weinberger, **Perspective On Social Welfare**, (San Diego, San Diego State College Press, 1969), p. 237.

CAUSE AND EFFECT RELATIONSHIPS

This discussion exercise provides practice in the skill of analyzing cause and effect relationships. Causes of human conflict and social problems are usually very complex. The following statements indicate possible causes for welfare abuses. Rank them by assigning the number (1) to the most important cause, number (2) to the second most important, and so on until the ranking is finished. Omit any statements you feel are not causative factors. Add any causes you think have been left out. Then discuss and compare your decisions with other class members.

_____ a. The weakness of human nature and its tendency to avoid work and effort.

_____ b. The bureaucratic inefficiency of government welfare programs that encourage cheating.

_____ c. The indifference and lack of dedication of welfare case workers.

_____ d. The "something for nothing" attitude that exists in American society.

_____ e. The apathy of the public.

_____ f. The lack of harsh punishment for those found guilty of welfare fraud.

_____ g. The breakdown of morals in our society.

_____ h. Communists' efforts to undermine our society.

THE ESSENTIAL IDEA
OF THE WELFARE STATE

by the Chamber of Commerce of the U.S.*

The Chamber of Commerce of the United States is a
national federation of voluntary organizations of
business and professional men. It attempts to make
known to the public and the government the recommendations of the business community on national
issues. It was founded in 1912 and currently has
several publications, including the monthly, **Nation's
Business."**

Consider these questions as you read:

1. Why does the Chamber of Commerce feel that the
   individual's income depends less and less on his
   own efforts in the welfare state?
2. How does this reading attempt to point out that the
   Constitution does not support the expansion of the
   welfare state?
3. What does the Chamber of Commerce feel are the
   long range effects of the welfare state?

*****The Welfare State and the State of Human Welfare**, by the Committee on
Economic Policy of the Chamber of Commerce of the United States, 1950.

"To go back to the good old days" is neither practical nor desirable. But every new idea or proposal is not necessarily good because it is new. Established ideas and values may be well worth preserving and even strengthening. The Welfare State, as we will see, represents a distinct departure from much that we have found good in the past. It will bring on, in the judgment of many individuals, some inevitable consequences for our economic and political life that all of us would want to avoid. . . .

THE ESSENTIAL IDEA IN THE WELFARE STATE

In its major aspect, the Welfare State is one in which the individual's income depends less and less on his own efforts. The Welfare State progressively weakens the tie between the individual's income and his economic contribution to society. This is accomplished, broadly, in two ways:

1. The state imposes heavier taxes on more productive individuals and subsidizes those of lower productivity.

2. The state sets up areas or sectors of protection, semiprivate preserves, free from the rigors of competitive price determination.

In pre-welfare state periods, it was considered just and proper that each individual should get the benefit of his own efforts and achievements; a system of incentives and rewards was recognized as leading to maximum human welfare. A primary duty of the state was to restrain fraud and violence and keep the economy competitive. Under the Welfare State, the earnings of the more productive and efficient individuals are tapped for the benefit of the less productive and less efficient. The state becomes the instrument to effectuate this transfer of income from the one group to another.

Clearly, this constitutes a fundamental revolution in the theory of government and of the state. Once the full import of this change is grasped, it is certain to challenge our thoughtfulness. . . .

THE WELFARE STATE AND THE CONSTITUTION

The welfare statist often quotes the Constitution to justify the expansion of the state. President Truman, for example, in support of one of his programs, recently said:

"For many generations we have recognized that there is a legitimate role for the government to play in protecting our people from economic injustice and hardship. Our founding fathers explicitly stated this. In the Preamble to the Constitution of the United States, it is declared that this government was established among other reasons 'to promote the general welfare'."

In so saying, the President not only misquoted the Constitution, but reinterpreted it to make it appear to conform to the idea of the Welfare State. Actually, what the Preamble says is that We . . . the people . . . in order to . . . promote the general welfare . . . establish *this Constitution* . . ." The *Constitution,* not the government, was established to attain these goals.

This distinction is fundamental. The founding fathers aimed to establish a general framework, a set of broad rules within which human beings would function and operate, as individuals, as groups, and sometimes even as government. There is a vast difference, however, between setting up a government to do things for the individual and setting up a constitutional system within which individuals could do things for themselves and for each other.

The United States Supreme Court, furthermore, has repeatedly held that the Preamble of the Constitution in no sense confers any authority for government action, either state or Federal. It is the subsequent part of the Constitution which allocates power and authority. The founding fathers assigned to Congress only 17 groups of powers (Article 3, Sec. 8). Congress has these powers and no others. Technically, Congress cannot even pass laws to promote the general welfare! Every law it passes must be based on one or another of specific, enumerated powers.

Of course, no one would argue that the Constitution cannot be changed. But if the welfare statists mean to channel our society further down the road of statism, many individuals feel that they should call a constitutional convention to scrap what we have and pave the way in legal and constitutional fashion for the transformation which they wish to accomplish. . . .

MORAL AND ECONOMIC RATIONALE

Throughout our Anglo-Saxon history and traditions, there has always run a limited but definite equalitarian

WELFARE STATE
BLUNDERS

1. Federal regulation of agriculture was supposed to save the small farms and slow the flow of population to the cities. The result has been a subsidy system that promotes large farms, penalizes small farms, and stimulates the flow of population into the cities, where the poor buy food at high prices which the Federal Government supports using their tax revenues.

2. Minimum wage laws are supposed to aid marginal workers by improving upon market forces. But I know of no economist who does not acknowledge that such wage laws produce unemployment among marginal workers, especially among young blacks.

3. Regulation of trucking keeps freight rates high. Regulation of air travel keeps ticket prices high, thereby restricting the mobility of the population. Regulation of the railroads has made them what they are today.

4. The state monopoly of the postal services has helped make the penny postcard what it is today. This monopoly is backed by an astonishing law that makes private enterprise in postal services a federal crime. Lacking such a law, the state monopoly would be without business.

5. Federal housing projects have resulted in an increase in slums and a decrease in the number of housing units available to the poor.

6. Rent control was imposed in New York as a putative wartime necessity. Like all such laws, rent control will exist forever. That rent control creates slums is obvious to every thinking man who has studied the subject. . . .

7. Today there are ten times more government agencies dealing with the problems of the cities than there were in 1939. But who believes the cities are better off — let alone ten times better off — than they were in 1939?

8. In Washington, D.C. liberal judges have concocted enough laws, and federal sociologists have concocted enough theories, to rationalize the nation's most ambitious integration policy. The result is that Washington schools are 95 per cent black — the least integrated in the nation.

George F. Wills, *The Welfare State: Boob-bait for McGovernites*, **National Review**, July 7, 1972, p. 735. Reprinted with permission from **National Review**.

strain. We have always taken care of people "in need", a term now taking on new elasticity! The Declaration of Independence emphasizes that we are all created equal. The Constitution prohibits class distinction based on hereditary titles. We reacted strongly against the feudal caste system. Early in our history we supported universal, common school education. *We were committed to the doctrine of the equal start.*

Later, this same set of ideas was commonly referred to as "equality of opportunity". We felt that if every child were educated, and there were no legal or other artificial barriers, we would all have this equal start. *Then each should be entitled to keep whatever he could earn.* . . .

LONG RANGE EFFECTS OF THE WELFARE STATE

The foregoing review indicates that the Welfare State has two basic characteristics: (1) It attempts to level and socialize income; (2) It attempts to set aside and negate the free market as the guide to production through controls, subsidies, government guarantees and a host of other devices.

This intervention fosters groupism, group conflict, and economic syndicalism.* While it attempts to provide protection, it steadily creates more rigidities, more immobility and, if this trend continues, it must end in a class society and a weakened industrial potential. . . .

THE END RESULTS OF THE WELFARE STATE

The Welfare State by its very nature tends to merge economics and politics, and join, rather than keep separate, the legislative, executive, and judicial branches of the government. It must rely for its existence on unlimited rather than limited government. If, as Thomas Hobbes has said, "Freedom is political power divided into small fragments," then freedom under the Welfare State is put in jeopardy.

The tyranny of the state has been demonstrated anew in our times in Italy, Germany, Russia and elsewhere. Democracies one after another have given way to the total state, with the state made responsible for welfare, for employment, for security. The politicians govern and control not only the traditional affairs of government, but also the economic system. Instead of dispersing and diffusing power and authority, the total drift of the Welfare State is toward the concentration of power and authority — toward the total state — totalitarianism.

*On the rising economic syndicalism see: **Economic Intelligence**, February, 1950. Chamber of Commerce of the United States.

MYTHS ABOUT WELFARE

by DEPARTMENT OF HEALTH, EDUCATION AND WELFARE*

This reading is taken from a pamphlet entitled **Welfare Myths vs. Facts**," published by the U.S. Department of Health, Education and Welfare." Its purpose, according to HEW, is "to explode some of the popular misconceptions," about welfare recipients.

Keep the following questions in mind as you read:

1. What proof does HEW offer to support its claim that welfare recipients are not lazy work dodgers?
2. Why does HEW claim that life on welfare is a difficult and hard existence?

*Department of Health, Education and Welfare, **Welfare Myths vs. Facts**. Publication (SRS) 72-02009. Unfortunately this pamphlet is out of print.

MYTH: **WELFARE FAMILIES ARE LOADED WITH KIDS — AND HAVE MORE KIDS JUST TO GET MORE MONEY.**

HEW's REPLY: The typical welfare family has a mother and three children. Since 1967, the trend has been toward smaller families on welfare. The birth rate for welfare families, like the birth rate for the general population, is dropping.

Most children in welfare families — 90 per cent — are 2 years old or older. Studies show that the average family receives assistance for about two years. It is clear, then, that the majority of welfare children were conceived or born before the family applied for assistance. Also, the typical payment for an additional child is $35 a month, hardly enough to cover the cost of rearing an additional child. Some States impose maximum-payment limits; families reaching that ceiling — usually a four to five-person family — get no additional money for another child.

MYTH: **MOST WELFARE FAMILIES ARE BLACK.**

HEW's REPLY: The largest racial group among welfare families — 49 per cent — is white.

Blacks represent about 46 per cent. Most of the remaining 5 per cent are American Indians, Orientals and other racial minorities. Latin-American families cut across racial lines; 14.4 per cent of AFDC (aid to families with dependent children) families are of Latin birth or ancestry: Mexican, Cuban, Venezuelan, etc.

MYTH: **YOU CAN LIVE WELL ON WELFARE.**

HEW's REPLY: The average payment to a welfare family of four with no other income varies among States, from a low of $60 per month in Mississippi to a high of $375 per month in Alaska.

In all but four States, welfare payments have been below the established poverty level of $331 per month, or $3,972 per year for a family of four. Unfortunately, some of the nation's working poor — ineligible for assistance under the present welfare system — earn less than the poverty level, too.

Each State establishes its own ''need standard'' — the amount required for the necessities of family living. A State standard may be below or above the poverty line. A State will use its need standard as a base for determining eligibility. However, 38 States pay less — some much less — than their own established standard of need. The Federal Government shares the cost of payments made by the States.

Welfare-reform proposals — establishing a federal income floor nationally for welfare families — would provide an even base for payments and increase recipients' incomes in at least eight States now paying the lowest amounts. The working poor would get a cash assist as well, insuring that a family head would always be better off by working. Under welfare reform, any family head who is able to work but remains unemployed would have to take a job or job training in order to receive welfare benefits.

MYTH: **GIVE WELFARE RECIPIENTS MORE MONEY AND THEY'LL SPEND IT ON DRINK AND BIG CARS.**

HEW's REPLY: Most welfare families report that if they received any extra money it would go for essentials.

A survey of welfare mothers showed that almost half would spend it primarily for food. Anther 28 per cent said they would spend any additional money on clothing and shoes. The survey found that 42 per cent of mothers bought used clothing or relied on donated clothing to help make ends meet. Seventeen per cent of the mothers said their children occasionally stayed home from school because they lacked decent clothes and shoes. Nearly 10 per cent of the mothers in the survey said they would spend extra money on rent for better housing, and 13 per cent said they would spend it on a combination of food, clothes and rent.

MYTH: **MOST WELFARE CHILDREN ARE ILLEGITI-MATE.**

HEW's REPLY: a sizable majority — approximately 68 per cent — of the more than 7 million children in welfare families were born in wedlock, according to data compiled by the Social and Rehabilitation Service.

In addition, most middle and upper-income families have always been able to purchase family-planning counseling and services from private physicians. However, only in the past few years has government made a concerted effort to deliver such services to the poor.

MYTH: **ONCE ON WELFARE, ALWAYS ON WELFARE.**

HEW's REPLY: The average welfare family has been on the rolls for 23 months.

Studies by the Social and Rehabilitation Service, HEW, show that at any given time about two thirds of welfare families will have been receiving assistance for less than three years. The number of long-term cases is relatively small — only 7.3 per cent have been on welfare for 10 years or more. Such cases are likely to involve some form of disability.

The welfare scapegoat

Government-sponsored surveys show that the majority of welfare families are also embarrassed by and discontented with welfare. Most want to move off the welfare rolls, but it takes the average family about two years to overcome its problems.

Proposed welfare reforms are designed to strengthen work incentives, eliminate barriers to employment, and thus help present recipients rejoin the work force as soon as possible.

MYTH: **WELFARE PEOPLE ARE CHEATS.**

HEW's REPLY: Suspected incidents of fraud or misrepresentation among welfare recipients occur in less than four tenths of 1 per cent of the total welfare case load in the nation, according to all available evidence. Cases where fraud is established occur even less frequently.

Another 1 to 2 per cent of welfare cases are technically ineligible because of a misunderstanding of the rules, agency mistakes, or changes in family circumstances not reported fast enough. These are human and technical errors; it is not cheating.

While the proportion of those who deliberately falsify information is very low, both the federal and State governments seek to eliminate them from the welfare rolls as well as to remove all errors in determining eligibility. The overwhelming majority of recipients, like most other Americans, are not wilfully misrepresenting their situations.

State agencies are required to check the eligibility of AFDC families at least once every six months; those with unemployed fathers, once every three months. The Federal Government also analyzes State records and makes on-site checks of a portion of each State's welfare cases.

Many publicized charges of cheating or ineligibility simply have not stood up under investigation

MYTH: **THE WELFARE ROLLS ARE FULL OF ABLE-BODIED LOAFERS.**

HEW's REPLY: Less than 1 per cent of welfare recipients are able-bodied, unemployed males; some 126,000 of the more than 13 million Americans on federal-State-supported welfare (April, 1971, statistics). Most of them — 80 per cent — want work, according to a Government-sponsored study; about half the men are enrolled in work-training programs.

The largest group of working-age adults on welfare are 2.5 million mothers of welfare families, most of whom head families with no able-bodied male present. About 14 per cent of these mothers work, and 7 per cent are in work training.

Many of the other mothers confront serious barriers to employment under the existing welfare system. But if day care were available for their children and if job training and jobs were to be had it is estimated that another 35 per cent would be potential employes.

An additional 4 to 5 per cent of mothers have some employment potential, but require more extensive social rehabilitative service to prepare them. The proposed welfare-reform program includes provisions for day care, job training, public-service jobs and more extensive service for welfare recipients.

The remaining 40 per cent of welfare mothers have little or no employment potential because they care for small children at home, have major physical or mental incapacities, or other insurmountable work barriers. In spite of this, 70 to 80 per cent of welfare mothers consistently report they would work if present barriers to employment are overcome.

ABILITY TO DISCRIMINATE

   Usually difficult situations fail to present easy choices. Real life problems are too complex to permit simple choices between absolute right and wrong. The following exercises will test your ability to discriminate between degrees of truth and falsehood by completing the questionnaire. Circle the number on the continuum which most closely identifies your evaluation regarding each statement's degree of truth or falsehood.

1. The rich and the affluent in our society receive more welfare benefits than the poor.

   + $\dfrac{\quad 5\quad 4\quad 3\quad 2\quad 1\quad 0\quad 1\quad 2\quad 3\quad 4\quad 5\quad}{\ }$ −

   | completely | partially | partially | completely |
   | true | true | false | false |

2. The welfare rolls are full of able-bodied loafers.

   + $\dfrac{\quad 5\quad 4\quad 3\quad 2\quad 1\quad 0\quad 1\quad 2\quad 3\quad 4\quad 5\quad}{\ }$ −

   | completely | partially | partially | completely |
   | true | true | false | false |

3. Welfare programs place unfair demands on those who work and pay taxes to support them.

+ ___5__4__3__2__1__0__1__2__3__4__5___ —
    completely   partially   partially   completely
       true   true   false   false

4. The average American is too proud to accept welfare assistance when in need.

+ ___5__4__3__2__1__0__1__2__3__4__5___ —
    completely   partially   partially   completely
       true   true   false   false

5. An advanced welfare state, such as Sweden's, would not work in our country.

+ ___5__4__3__2__1__0__1__2__3__4__5___ —
    completely   partially   partially   completely
       true   true   false   false

6. Replacing our present welfare programs with a negative income tax would benefit everyone.

+ ___5__4__3__2__1__0__1__2__3__4__5___ —
    completely   partially   partially   completely
       true   true   false   false

IS WELFARE A BASIC HUMAN RIGHT?

by Milton Friedman*

Milton Friedman in a nationally known economist who writes a regular column for **Newsweek**. He is also the author of many books and a frequent contributor to a large number of journals. He has an extensive background as an educator and currently teaches in the department of economics of the University of Chicago.

As you read consider the following questions?

1. What does Mr. Friedman claim is the cause of most hardship and misery in the U.S.?
2. What is the unacceptable result of a person's having a right to food, clothing, shelter and medical care?
3. What is Mr. Friedman's suggested alternative to our current welfare programs?

*Milton Friedman, Is Welfare a Basic Right? **Newsweek**, December 18, 1972, p. 90. Copyright **Newsweek**, Inc., 1972, Reprinted by Permission.

In a recent **Newsweek** column on poverty, Shana Alexander wrote, "Access to food, clothing, shelter and medical care is a basic human right."

The heart approves Ms. Alexander's humanitarian concern, but the head warns that her statement admits of two very different meanings, one that is consistent with a free society, and one that is not.

THE RIGHT TO WORK

One meaning is that everyone should be free to use his human capacities to acquire food, clothing, shelter and medical care by either direct production or voluntary cooperation with others. This meaning is the essence of a free society organized through voluntary cooperation.

This meaning is far from trivial. Indeed, I conjecture that most hardship and misery in the U.S. today reflect government's interference with this right. You cannot earn your livelihood by becoming a plumber, barber, mortician, lawyer, physician, dentist, or by entering a host of other trades, unless you first are licensed by the government. And the granting of a license is typically in the hands of practitioners of the trade you desire to enter, who find it in their self-interest to restrict entry.

You will have difficulty getting a highly paid job as a carpenter, mason or electrician unless you can persuade a union to let you join, and that may not be easy if your brother or father or uncle is not a member of the union. It will be especially difficult if you are black and poor, however competent. Like the American Medical Association, the unions can enforce their tight monopoly only with the support of the government.

If you are a black teen-ager whose services are currently worth only $1.50 an hour, it is illegal for most employers to hire you, even though you are willing to accept that wage.

And I have only scratched the surface of existing restrictions on your basic human right to use your capacities as you wish, provided only that you do not interfere with the right of others to do the same.

But this is not Ms. Alexander's meaning, as is clear from her next sentence: "When lawmakers attempt to convert welfare into workfare . . . this is less conversion that perversion of that basic idea."

Ms. Alexander apparently believes that you and I have a "basic human right" to food, clothing, shelter and medical care without a quid pro quo. That is a very different matter.

If I have the "right" to food in this sense, someone must have the obligation to provide it. Just who is that? If it is Ms. Alexander, does that not convert her into my slave? Nothing is changed by assigning the "right" to the "poor." Their "right" is meaningless unless it is combined with the power to force others to provide the goods to which Ms. Alexander believes they are entitled.

This is clearly unacceptable. But neither can we rely solely on the "right to access" in the first sense. Protecting that right fully would reduce poverty and destitution drastically. But there would still remain people who, through no fault of their own, because of accidents of birth, or illness, or whatever, were unable to earn what the rest of us would regard as an acceptable minimum income. I believe that the best, though admittedly imperfect, solution for such residual hardship would be voluntary action on the part of the rest of us to assist our less fortunate brethren.

TRANSITION PROGRAMS

But our problem is far more serious. Restrictions on access in the first sense, plus ill-conceived welfare measures, have made millions of people dependent on government for their most elementary needs. It was a mistake to have permitted this situation to develop. But it has developed, and we cannot simply wipe the slate clean. We must develop transition programs that eliminate the welfare mess without unconscionable hardship to present welfare recipients.

That is why, for three decades, I have urged the replacement of our present collection of so-called poverty programs by a negative income tax that would guarantee a minimum to everyone and would encourage recipients to become self-supporting.

I favor a negative income tax not because I believe anyone has a "right" to be fed, clothed and housed at someone else's expense but because I want to join my fellow taxpayers in relieving distress and feel a special compulsion to do so because governmental policies have been responsible for putting so many of our fellow citizens in the demeaning position in which they now find themselves.

THE SWEDISH WELFARE STATE

by Ake Fors*

Ake Fors is Head of Division at the Swedish Ministry of Health and Social Affairs. The following reading is taken from **Social Policy and How It Works**, published by the Swedish Institute.

Consider these questions as you read:

1. How did the Swedish welfare state develop?
2. What is the current Swedish view concerning community assistance to those in need?
3. How does Sweden feel that its affluence and high standard of living affects welfare assistance?

*Copies of the pamphlet from which this reading was taken, and additional pamphlets, may be obtained from the Swedish Institute, Hamngatan 27, P.O. Box 7072, S-103 82 Stockholm 7, Sweden, or from the Swedish embassy in Washington, D.C. **Social Policy and How It Works** was published in Sweden by Kugelbergs Boktryckeri AB, Stockholm in 1972.

HISTORY OF THE SWEDISH WELFARE STATE

In mediaeval Sweden, it was the task of the church to care for the poor and the sick, even if the community as such probably played its part in practice even at that time. In the 16th century, at the time of the Reformation, when the state appropriated the property of the church, responsibility was assumed also for the latter's institutions for the care of the poor and sick. The state, however, soon found this an excessive burden, and transferred responsibility to the parishes. The King-in-Council decreed that each parish should maintain a home by the church and there "sustain its sick and support its poor". Such activities, which were naturally of the most primitive type, were financed by charity. Around the middle of the 18th century it was decreed that the parish's care of the poor and sick should be financed by local taxes.

By this time there had emerged a certain division of responsibility, the counties answered for physical medical care at hospitals, while the state was responsible for mental care and the "open care" that was by then being provided by "provincial physicians", i.e. district medical officers, who offered health and medical services in their respective areas. The parishes answered for other care, i.e. mainly poor relief.

This division was confirmed upon the creation of the county councils in 1862, and subsequent changes have only increased the councils' responsibility for medical services. In the 1960's, the 25 county councils and the three largest cities assumed responsibility also for psychiatric care and the system of district medical officers. Health and medical services are in fact the primary function of the county councils, claiming about 80 per cent of the funds the councils acquire via taxation and, in some cases, supplementary state grants. The fact that the county councils have been able to concentrate on this task is probably the main reason why Sweden has more hospital beds available per 1,000 inhabitants than other countries. Since hospital care is practically free, these resources are utilized to a high degree; this has led to an attempt to balance the central status of the hospitals by increased efforts in the field of open care.

That the municipalities and county councils are immediately responsible for the care of the individual, for social assistance, and for health and medical services, is generally regarded as a great advantage. Both the municipalities and the county councils are taxing authorities, and are entirely independent within the framework of the legislation enacted by the government and Parliament. . . .

Children in difficulties, alcoholics and their families, the partially disabled, old people who cannot manage on their own — all these have the right to assistance and care by the local authority. The municipalities also provide various types of service. They are responsible, for instance, for home help services for the aged and handicapped, and for families with children who require temporary assistance, e.g. if the mother falls ill, for homes for the aged, day nurseries, etc., and recreational facilities of different kinds.

There are hardly any private hospitals in Sweden. Social welfare services are provided by voluntary organizations only in the largest towns, and on a minor scale. The Red Cross is active to some extent among old people, the Link Society works among alcoholics, and various organizations promote different kinds of leisure activity. There exist some 20 national organizations of and for different groups with physical or mental handicaps. These organizations play a large and growing role. . . .

A HOSPITAL OUTSIDE STOCKHOLM

From minimum benefit to protection of living standard

Social insurance in Sweden, the "national insurance", consists basically of four different insurances, namely sickness insurance, maternity insurance, the basic pension, and national supplementary pension. These have emerged one after the other, and are continuously being improved. They are now co-ordinated in a uniform and essentially simple organization.

The original idea of public national insurance was to guarantee all persons, regardless of income and employment, a uniform minimum standard. Subsequently, the more ambitious aim was adopted of supplementing this minimum protection with individually adjusted protection against loss of income. It is considered that an insured person who falls ill, becomes disabled, or retires from gainful employment by reason of old age should enjoy insurance benefits that will enable him by and large to maintain the standard of living to which he has previously been accustomed.

Steadily growing social responsibility

The trend in Sweden has been towards a steadily increasing responsibility on the part of the community for the social security of its citizens, and for the provision of increased social services. The division of responsibility between state, county council and municipality is partly historically determined, but there is a clear tendency to give the municipalities — which are closest to the individual — the direct responsibility for individual care. Development has not rendered voluntary contributions superfluous. Such efforts are needed as a supplement to those of the

---

EVERYONE HAS A RIGHT TO HELP

The Swedish view is that everyone has the *right* to help from the community when they need it. Voluntary efforts can only supplement those of the community, and their value lies precisely in offering something beyond the routine. But charities must never be an excuse for public neglect, or delay efforts financed by taxation. Only public services based on public taxation can be the legislated right of all citizens.

community. Just as there is agreement today as regards the community's responsibility for social security, so too there is agreement as to the value of personal commitments and close personal contacts between different groups of people in the society.

The need for security increases with affluence

The expansion of the social services system has afforded an experience that would previously have appeared paradoxical, namely that the individual's demand for security and social care rises with his affluence. Once a high standard of living has been achieved, there is more reason to aim at greater security rather than further increases in standard. The man who has much to lose has correspondingly much to protect, and he wants a guarantee that he will not find himself in financial difficulties that may devastate his home and family life. This is confirmed by the way in which the scope of supplementary insurance policies provided by private companies has increased parallel with the development of national insurance. We can also say that the general view of social security has altered. Previously, such measures were regarded purely as a burden on the economy of central and local government. Today, social policy is regarded as an important positive factor in that it offers the individual not only greater security but also a greater chance of making an active contribution in production and the life of the community. In other words, it is considered that social policy pays off in the national economy.

Care and support during sickness

Swedish medical care is organized and paid for predominantly by the public sector. By the terms of the Medical Care Act, the county councils shall provide for those domiciled in their areas both non-institutionalized and institutionalized care for diseases, injuries, physical defects and childbirth. The county councils run their health and medical services independently, exacting taxes for this purpose from the local population.

The Swedish national insurance is compulsory and covers all persons over the age of 16 who are resident in the country, and their children.

A person who falls ill and visits a doctor within the noninstitutionalized public system (a hospital physician, district medical officer, or doctor on call) pays SKr 7 if he calls on the doctor at his surgery, SKr 15 if the doctor visits him at home.) The social insurance office does not reimburse this charge, but pays the rest of the cost of the visit directly to the responsible authority (usually the county council).

For the above-mentioned fee the patient will also receive any X-ray and laboratory examinations. The fee also covers referrals, prescriptions, and medical certificates for the purposes of sickness benefit. If the patient requires a whole series of X-ray or radium treatments, he will also receive these without further cost. If, for instance, the patient is referred by a district medical officer to a specialist at a hospital department, he will not be required to make any further payment for his first visit to the specialist. Further visits to a doctor are paid for as new visits.

A DOCTOR'S OFFICE

A person using a private practitioner pays the doctor's entire fee. He then presents the receipt to the insurance office, which will reimburse him to three quarters of the total cost in accordance with a special list of charges. . . .

Travel to a doctor is reimbursed by the insurance office, except for SKr 6, which the patient himself pays. Patients must travel in the cheapest manner possible in view of their medical state. Those who are hospitalized receive back the entire cost of travel.

A person who falls ill and reports his illness to the social insurance office receives a sickness benefit, which is designed to compensate him for loss of income during his illness. The amount of sickness benefit thus depends on the income lost. Housewives (and men of equivalent status), who do not lose any income, receive a basic sickness benefit of SKr 6 per day.

Dental care required by reason of illness is reimbursed to 3/4 of the cost. Expectant mothers, and those who have just given birth, receive compensation for dental care to 3/4 of the cost, in accordance with a special list of charges.

The county councils provide care under the national dental service, which primarily covers children between the ages of 6 and 16, in certain cases 3 and 5. These are treated free of charge. Adults, too, can receive dental care in so far as resources are available, paying in accordance with a special list of charges. In 1970, about one million children and over half a million adults were treated under the national dental service.

A proposal on dental insurance is to be presented to Parliament in 1973. A commission is currently studying how a practical insurance scheme of this kind should be structured. A necessary condition for dental insurance will be the reinforcement of the national dental service's resources. . . .

Measures on behalf of the aged

Modern care of the aged can be said to have three main functions, namely to offer elderly people financial independence, good housing, and such personal care as may be required.

By and large, it is the state that answers for financial support to the aged. A person who has reached the age of 67 is entitled to an old-age pension under the national basic pensions scheme. This pension is a basic benefit paid to all persons, regardless of previous earned income.

Approximately half of all pensioners receive housing allowances to supplement their old-age pension, these being subject to a means test. The sum in question is determined and paid by the municipal authorities, and covers to an increasing extent the actual housing costs of pensioners. A person living exclusively on the basic old-age pension plus housing allowance is not required to pay any income tax. . . .

HOBBY ROOM IN A HOME FOR THE AGED

A person who by reason of a lasting illness or handicap has completely lost his working capacity is entitled to a disability pension from the national basic pensions scheme. . . .

The general thinking in Sweden is that old people should be offered an opportunity to remain in their homes, in their accustomed environment, as long as they can manage. Only when the requirement for care reaches a stage at which it cannot be met by assistance in the home should the question of institutional care arise. In accordance with this view, the public sector supports the improvement of old people's housing and makes assistance in the home available.

A pensioner living in a poorly equipped dwelling, and unable to improve it by his own resources, can obtain state support for limited improvements, including water and

104

drainage facilities, water-closet, heat insulation, heating facilities and improved kitchen equipment. Since 1964, over 100,000 dwellings mainly in county districts, have been improved in these respects.

For the old and handicapped to be able to continue living in their homes, even when they have wholly or partially lost the capacity to perform daily routine tasks, the municipalities have organized assistance in the form of visitors or "Home Samaritans". The state helps to finance such services, by paying 35 per cent of the municipalities' actual costs. The tasks of a Home Samaritan include assisting with shopping, cooking, cleaning and other domestic tasks. Severely sick or handicapped old people can receive assistance every day, others perhaps need help only once or twice a week. Those living exclusively on the basic old-age pension receive such help free of charge. Others pay a small charge, which is related to income. . . .

Support to families with children

Support by the public sector to families with children is provided in the form of both cash benefits and services.

The main form of financial support to such families is the general children's allowances, which comprise SKr 1,200 per year for each child under 16. These allowances are paid quarterly, and are tax-free.

Central and local government housing allowances are an important supplement to the children's allowances for families with a low income, and those with several children. Almost half of Swedish families with children receive a state housing allowance, to a varying sum. It is estimated that some 90 per cent of single parents receive such an allowance. Housing allowances are subject to a means test, and can be paid to families with one or more children under 17 living at home. . . .

Preschools and free-time centres

Preschool and free-time centres have developed in Sweden as an integral part of the child welfare system. The preschool has two parts, namely the day nurseries, which are open 11 — 12 hours a day 5 — 6 days per week, and the playschools, which provide three hours of activity per child per day for five days a week. The free-time centres are day nurseries for schoolchildren, primarily those in the 7 — 9 age group. . . .

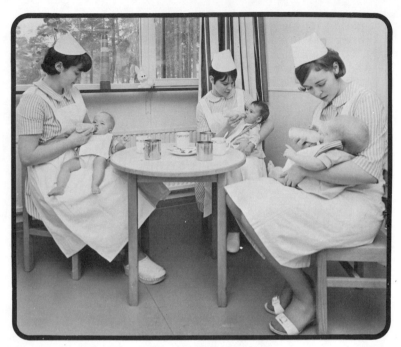

A DAYCARE CENTER

Help in education

Schooling is free in the compulsory comprehensive schools (9 years), secondary schools (2 — 4 years), and Folk High Schools (residential adult education schools). Higher education at universities and colleges is also free. Several lines of education at university level (e.g. medical studies) are subject to a *numerous clausus*, i.e. only a specific number of students can be accepted.

Students receive free school meals, free school books and other materials in the majority of compulsory schools, and in certain higher schools.

Young people over 16 who still attend the compulsory comprehensive receive an "extended children's allowance" of SKr 900 per year. Students between 16 and 19 attending secondary schools receive a study allowance of SKr 900 per year, in addition to which those between 17 and 19 can obtain, subject to a means test, an additional allowance of maximum SKr 75 per month during the school-year. If the student lives away from home while studying, he receives a lodging allowance of SKr 125 per month. In other cases, travel allowances can be made. . . .

The main purpose of social support for studies is to remove the remaining financial obstacles that prevent young people from acquiring the education and training they desire, and which the community can provide. It has also been considered important to make it easier for adults with short and inadequate schooling to improve their level of knowledge. Publically supported adult education is now on a considerable scale. . . .

WOMAN USING FACILITIES IN HER SPECIALLY CONSTRUCTED APARTMENT FOR THE HANDICAPPED

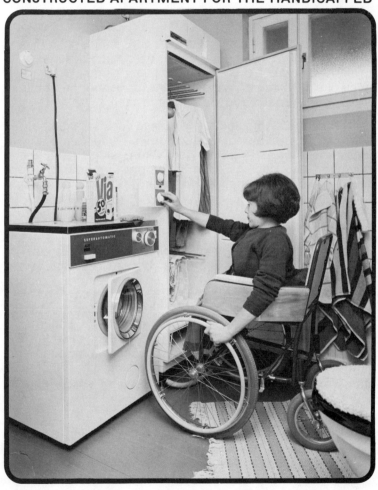

Support to the handicapped

Handicapped persons who have reached the age of 16 — the blind, orthopaedically handicapped, mentally retarded, etc. — receive a disability pension under the national basic pensions scheme, if they have lost their working capacity by reason of their handicap. . . .

A person who has not lost his entire working capacity — but at least 50 per cent — receives 2/3 or half the disability pension. . . .

Social assistance

Individually paid social assistance, subject to a means test, is provided by the municipalities. Such assistance is given when other aid cannot be obtained (either from insurance or elsewhere) or is insufficient, or cannot be obtained promptly. The usual form is a grant in cash. . . .

Those receiving social assistance consist largely of the sick and unemployed, single mothers, and families with many children. In the last ten years, single and young persons have increased their proportion among those receiving social assistance more than within the total population. . . .

Labour market policy

The public employment service is at the disposal of employers and job seekers alike. Its services include the handling of vacancies in all occupational sectors. Employment services are free of charge. Private employment services on a commercial basis (i.e. against payment by the applicant or employer) are forbidden in law. Thanks to a special system of notices, the local employment offices have a good overall picture of vacancies throughout the country. Contacts between job applicants and employers are established also by press advertising, particularly in the white collar sector.

State grants are paid to labour that is obliged to transfer to another district to obtain employment. Compensation is paid for travel and moving costs, plus a starting allowance to cover the first weeks' living expenses, and support to such families as are obliged for some time to maintain two places of domicile. In certain areas, the employment service also assists in buying up the houses of those who obtain work elsewhere.

108

In the majority of Western European countries, social insurance has developed mainly as employee insurance, in close association with labour legislation. In Sweden, on the other hand, social security is based on the principle of public national insurance. Everyone has the right to compensation in the event of sickness, and everyone is entitled to a pension on retirement or, in the event of disablement or the death of the family provider, even earlier.

Unemployed or recently handicapped persons often need training for a new occupation. The labour market authorities therefore organize "labour market training", which in any given year covers almost three per cent of the labour force. While training is in progress, both the trainee and his or her family receive a grant. . . .

Employees have the right to paid holiday, regardless of whether they are employed by central or local government authorities, private companies or individual employers. The right to a paid holiday is guaranteed by law, and the employee is eligible for two days' paid holiday if he has worked for a minimum of 15 days during a given month. The total number of days' paid holiday during the year is thus 24, which with Sundays means 4 weeks' holiday. Work for a minimum of 8 days during a given month confers the right to 1 day's paid holiday.

A WELFARE PROGRAM
FOR THE U.S.

by the Committee for Economic Development*

The Committee for Economic Development is composed of 200 leading businessmen and educators. One of its stated objectives is "to develop, through objective research and discussion, findings and recommendations for business and public policy which will contribute to the preservation and strengthening of our free society, and to the maintenance of high employment, increasing productivity and living standards, greater economic stability and greater opportunity for all our people." The following reading is taken from a statement on national policy by the Research and Policy Committee of the CED.

The following questions should help your understanding of the reading:

1. According to the CED, what major group of Americans is presently barred from participation in the welfare system?
2. What specific recommendations does the CED make to improve our country's welfare program?

***Improving the Public Welfare System**, Committee for Economic Development, April 1970, pp 18-22. This 75 page booklet can be obtained for $1.00 from the Committee for Economic Development, Distribution Division, 477 Madison .Ave., New York 10022.

SUMMARY OF RECOMMENDATIONS

Following are the recommendations made by this Committee in seeking ways to extend public assistance to *all* Americans living in want — a goal having high priority among the many goals being sought by this nation.

Barred from participation in the welfare system, without access to whatever benefits it does confer, are millions of Americans living on a subsistence level. The major group excluded from receiving public assistance are those who participate in the labor force, even though only part-time or at very low levels of pay. Such a disqualification in itself is not only unjust but also works against the establishment of a sound national policy that might eventually lead to the eradication of poverty. **We recommend a federally-supported program to provide a national minimum income with eligibility determined solely on the basis of need, whether need results from inadequate earnings or inability to work.** Also, **we recommend specifically the inclusion of working single-person families and working childless couples in any new federally-aided programs designed to benefit the poor.**

We believe that the assurance of a minimum income must be coupled with arrangements that provide strong incentives to work for all who are capable of work or of being trained for work. **We urge that a program of income incentives to work should be made a basic component of any new welfare system, coupled with positive measures to increase opportunities for private or public employment for those able to work.** The measures needed for accomplishing this will be discussed in the aforementioned statement on poverty and jobs under preparation by a CED Subcommittee on Problems of Urban Poverty.

The question arises whether, in addition to income incentives, a training or work requirement for those who are able to work is either a desirable or practicable feature of an income maintenance program. As a matter of principle, we believe that those who are able to work should work, and that even though such a requirement is difficult to apply, the principle should not be abrogated on that account. **We recommend the incorporation of a requirement for training or work for the able-to-work as an integral element of any income maintenance system provided that a proper manpower program is developed to make such a requirement meaningful and that safeguards are built into the organizational and appeals mechanisms to assure individual dignity and rights.**

In developing a national manpower and training program, we believe that special attention must be given to the problem of women who head households. This involves a consideration of whether the family's and society's longer-range interests are better served in individual instances by the presence of a mother in the home or by additional family income acquired through outside work. **We believe that neither training nor work should be made a condition for continuance of public assistance to women heads of households.**

PRESENT WELFARE SYSTEM IS 'OUTRAGE'

The present welfare system has become a monstrous, consuming outrage — an outrage against the community, against the taxpayer, and particularly against the children it is supposed to help.

We may honestly disagree, as we do, on what to do about it. But we can all agree that we must meet the challenge not by pouring more money into a bad program, but by abolishing the present system and adopting a new one.

State of the Union Address delivered before Congress on January 22, 1971, by President Nixon.

However, in order to facilitate jobholding where this is desirable, **we recommend the establishment of a federally-supported national program of day-care centers that will enable mothers receiving public assistance to augment their incomes through training and jobs. We also urge the development of a federal program to assist with the construction of day-care centers.**

Furthermore, **we strongly urge that the age of eligibility for inclusion in any such day-care program be extended down to include two-year-olds, and that the program should be broad in concept so that instead of being merely custodial in nature the centers provide an educational experience and enrichment for young children along the lines of Head Start.**

Since the evidence indicates that the number of children is much higher in poor families than among affluent families, we are concerned that family planning assistance be made available equally to all regardless of income. **We strongly urge that more money be provided, both to government and private agencies, so that family planning programs can be expanded in order to ensure that information is easily and readily available to all families.**

As we have stated, we believe that a uniform national approach to the problem of welfare is essential to the reform of the system. **We view as practical and realistic the proposal that the level of federal income maintenance be set to provide a minimum of $2,400 for a family of four at the present time.** The $2,400 figure for a family of four could consist of $1,600 in cash allotments with the remainder being provided through the Food Stamp Program, which we believe offers promise as a practical means for supplementing the nutrition of the poor. **We approve the use of the Food Stamp Program as additional to the welfare cash allotment and believe that it should be extended for the immediate future to all who qualify for income supplementation. However, we recommend that it be subject to periodic review and evaluation in order to ascertain whether the efficiency of the program can be improved and also whether cash payments might not better achieve the objectives of the program.**

Because the addition of the Food Stamp Program to the cash allotment has the effect of reducing the incentive for earnings, some changes would be required to preserve an adequate work incentive. **We recommend that in combining welfare cash and food subsidy programs for income maintenance, the incentive element be set so that the recipients retain an adequate percentage of earnings [centering around approximately half of earnings] above a minimum allowance [such as $720 a year] up to an appropriate cutoff point.**

Inasmuch as a minimum income of $2,400 for a family of four hardly provides a subsistence level of living, **we believe that a priority claim against future available federal funds should be invoked to raise total assistance to more acceptable levels.** Furthermore, as the minimum income is raised toward a more realistic level, regional distortions very likely will begin to occur. Therefore, **we recommend that as the minimum income level rises, consideration be given to adjustments for cost differentials where appropriate between various regions of the country and between urban and rural communities.**

A corollary of a truly uniform national system of public assistance based on income maintenance is that the federal government not only assume an increasing share of the necessarily increasing cost, but that it eventually undertake the entire burden. **As an objective to be attained as soon as fiscally feasible, we recommend that the federal government undertake a substantially higher proportion of the financing of public assistance with a phased takeover by the federal government of state and local public assistance costs over the next five years as the goal.**

Furthermore, **we recommend that as the federal government takes over responsibility for financing public** assistance payments, it likewise assume a commensurate responsibility for administering such assistance in order to assure efficiency as well as to provide all recipients equitable, uniform treatment.

It should be remembered that for the able-to-work, welfare is available only in the absence of a suitable job or job training. The present procedures for investigating and determining the qualifications of individuals for public assistance programs are not only demeaning but also cumbersome, costly, and time-consuming. The present system should be replaced by a far simpler and more direct method of certification by affidavit, which has now been adequately tested but which should be subject to periodic review. **We support the certification method of determining welfare eligibility for both federal and state portions of the system.**

Present methods of certification and payment are particularly onerous, needless and wasteful where the aged, blind, and disabled are concerned. **We recommend that the administration of the assistance programs for the aged, blind, and disabled be handled within the Department of Health, Education, and Welfare by federal payments in a manner similar to that used for Social Security payments.**

We are most concerned that adequate job and wage standards for determining initial and continuing eligibility of persons for public assistance be included in the training-job component of any proposed welfare system. **We recommend that a specific safeguard for the federal level be included to insure the following:**

a. Uniform local administration in determining eligibility in conformance with standards set by federal law, particularly those specifying wages and other conditions pertaining to a suitable job.

b. Prevention of punitive actions by local administrators in the termination of eligibility of local recipients.

c. Establishment of machinery for appeal of local administrative decisions concerning eligibility outside the administering local department, with details of these procedures clearly stated to each recipient.

IDENTIFYING THE POLITICAL POSITIONS OF INDIVIDUALS AND ORGANIZATIONS   EXERCISE 7

Although there is a danger in simplification and generalization, it can often be quite helpful to pigeonhole ideas, people, and organizations, particularly when one is trying to master new subject matter. It may be helpful to reread the introduction before starting this exercise.

Radical

— Individual freedom is an absolute
— The goal justifies the means
— Political idéals must not be compromised
— Belief in the economic system of Socialism

Liberal

— Reform by moderate means
— Expect the best of men
— Expanded role of federal government in solving social problems

Conservative

— Content with the present system
— Men need enlightened control
— The fewer government programs the better

Reactionary

— Traditional authority must be maintained
— All laws must be observed
— Political ideals must not be compromised
— Communism is the root of many problems

LEFT	10	9	8	7	6	5	4	3	2	1	0	1	2	3	4	5	6	7	8	9	10	RIGHT
	RADICAL				LIBERAL				MIDDLE-OF-ROAD				CONSERVATIVE				REACTIONARY			

116

1. Position the following individuals and organizations and present arguments to defend your placements: Hubert H. Humphrey, Juanita Kidd Stout, the Chamber of Commerce of the U.S. and the Department of Health, Education and Welfare.

2. Would the above four individuals and organizations be placed differently on the spectrum if they were examined in relation to their positions on American foreign policy rather than welfare?

3. What national organizations and famous personalities do you think could be easily positioned on the spectrum? Which would be difficult to position? Be able to give your reasons in each instance.

4. How would you position the following "isms" on the spectrum: Fascism, Socialism, Democracy, Capitalism, Communism?

APPENDIX A

PUBLICATIONS ON THE LEFT

ADA WORLD
(published by Americans for
  Democratic Action monthly)
1223 Connecticut Av e., N.W.
Washington, D.C. 20036

CHRISTIAN CENTURY
(published weekly)
407 So. Dearborn St.
Chicago, Ill.

CIVIL LIBERTIES
(published six times a year
  by the American Civil
  Liberties Union)
I56 Fifth Ave
New York, N.Y. 10010

COMMENTARY
(published monthly by the
  American Jewish
  Committee)
165 East 56th St.
New York, N.Y. I0022

I.F. STONE WEEKLY
(published weekly)
56I8 Nebraska Ave., Ave., N.W.
Washington, D.C. 20015

LID NEWS BULLETIN
(published irregularly by the
  League for Industrial
  Democracy)
112 E. 19th St.
New York, N.Y. I0003

NATION
(published weekly)
333 Sixth Ave.
New York, N.Y. I0014

**NATIONAL WELFARE LEADER
  NEWSLETTER**
(published semimonthly by the
  National Welfare Rights
  Organization)
1762   Corcoran, N.W.
Washington, D.C. 20036

NEW REPUBLIC
(published weekly)
1233 I9th St. N.W.
Washington, D.C. 20036

PROGRESSIVE
(published monthly)
408 W. Gorham
Madison, Wisconsin

APPENDIX B

PUBLICATIONS ON THE RIGHT

ACU REPORT
(published monthly by the
  American Conservative
  Union)
328 Pennsylvania Ave., S.E.
Washington, D.C. 20003

AMERICAN MERCURY
(published monthly by the
  John Birch Society)
395 Concord Ave.
Belmont, Mass. 02178

CHRISTIANITY TODAY
(published bi-weekly)
Washington Building
Washington, D.C. 20005

DAN SMOOT REPORT
(published weekly)
 p.o. Box 9538
Lakewood Station
Dallas, Texas 75214

HUMAN EVENTS
(published weekly)
422 First St., S.E.
Washington, D.C. 20003

LIBERTY LETTER
(published monthly during
  congressional sessions by
  Liberty Lobby)
300 Independence Ave., S.E.
Washington, D.C. 20003

NATIONAL REVIEW
(published bi-weekly)
150 E. 5th St.
New York, N.Y. 10016

THE NEW GUARD
(published monthly by
  Young Americans for
  Freedom, Inc.)
1221 Massachusetts Ave. N.W.
Washington, D.C. 20005

U.S. NEWS AND WORLD REPORT
(published weekly)
2300 N. St. N.W.
Washington, D.C. 20037

ACKNOWLEDGMENTS

Page

24   Fred O. Seibel in the Richmond **Times-Dispatch.** Reprinted with permission from the Richmond **Times-Dispatch**

31   Norris in the **Vancouver sun.** Reprinted with permission from the **Vancouver sun**

37   Justus in the **Minneapolis Star.** Reprinted with permission from the **Minneapolis Star**

45   Reprinted with permission of Construction Action, Inc.

57   Reprinted with permission from Liberty Lobby

72   Justus in the **Minneapolis Star.** Reprinted with permission from the **Minneapolis Star**

89   Scott Long in the **Minneapolis Tribune.** Reprinted with permission from the **Minneapolis Tribune**

99   Swedish Information Service

102   Swedish Information Service

104   Swedish Information Service

106   Swedish Information Service

107   Swedish Information Service

113   Justus in the **Minneapolis Star.** Reprinted with permission from the **Minneapolis Star**

MEET THE EDITOR

DAVID L. BENDER is a history graduate from the University of Minnesota. He also has an M.A. in government from St. Mary's University in San Antonio, Texas. He has taught social problems at the high school level for the past several years and is currently working on additional volumes for the Opposing Viewpoints Series.